I0824079

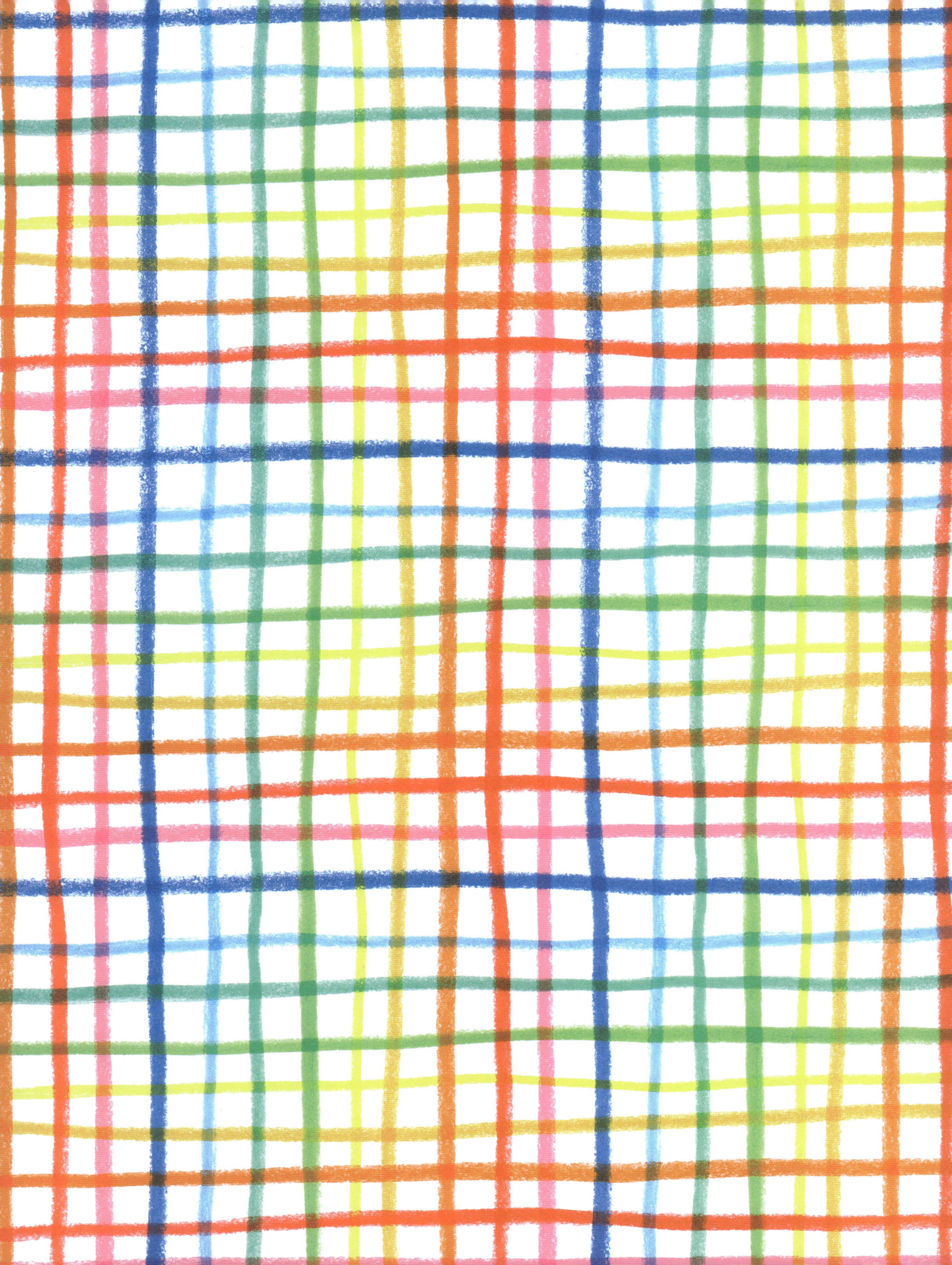

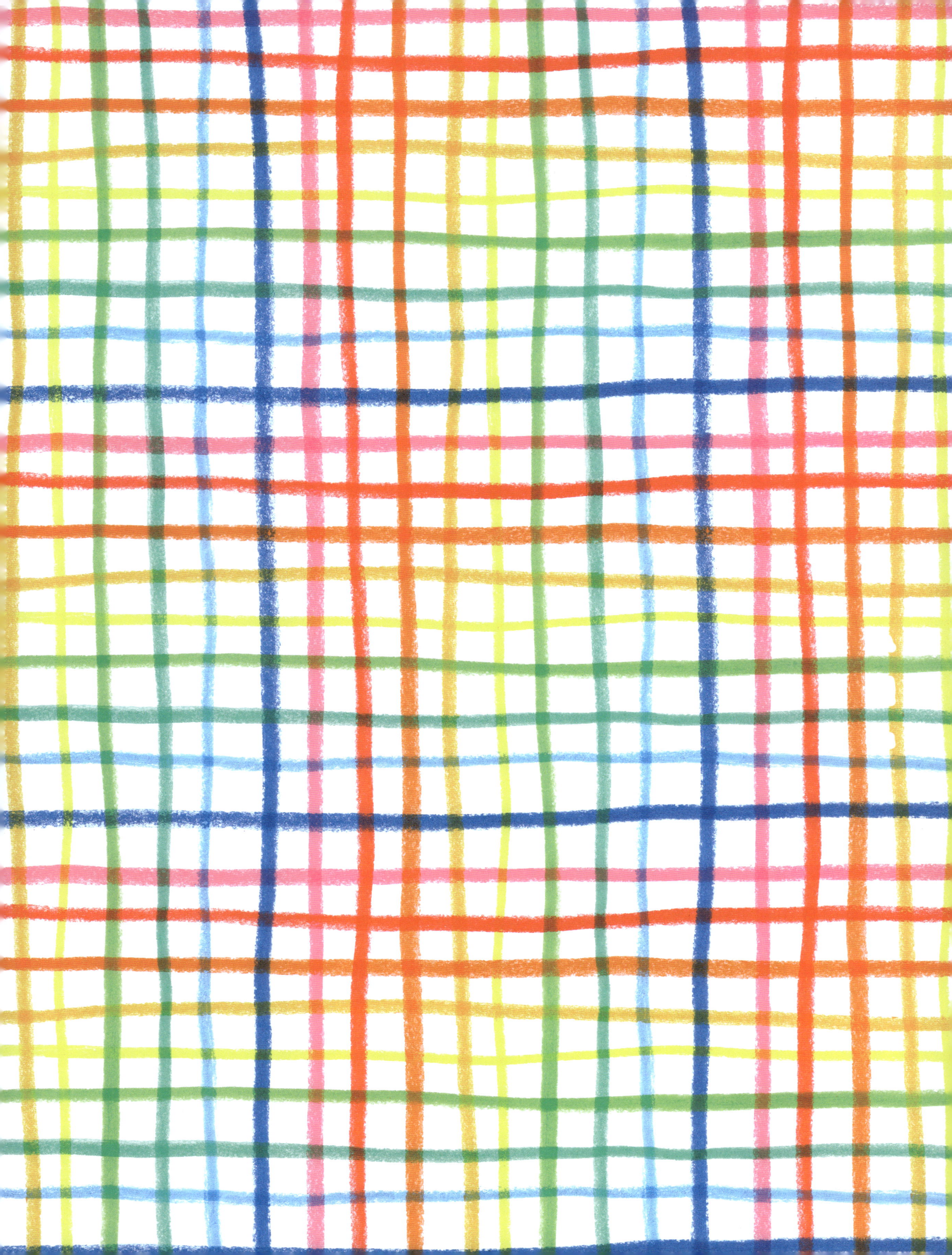

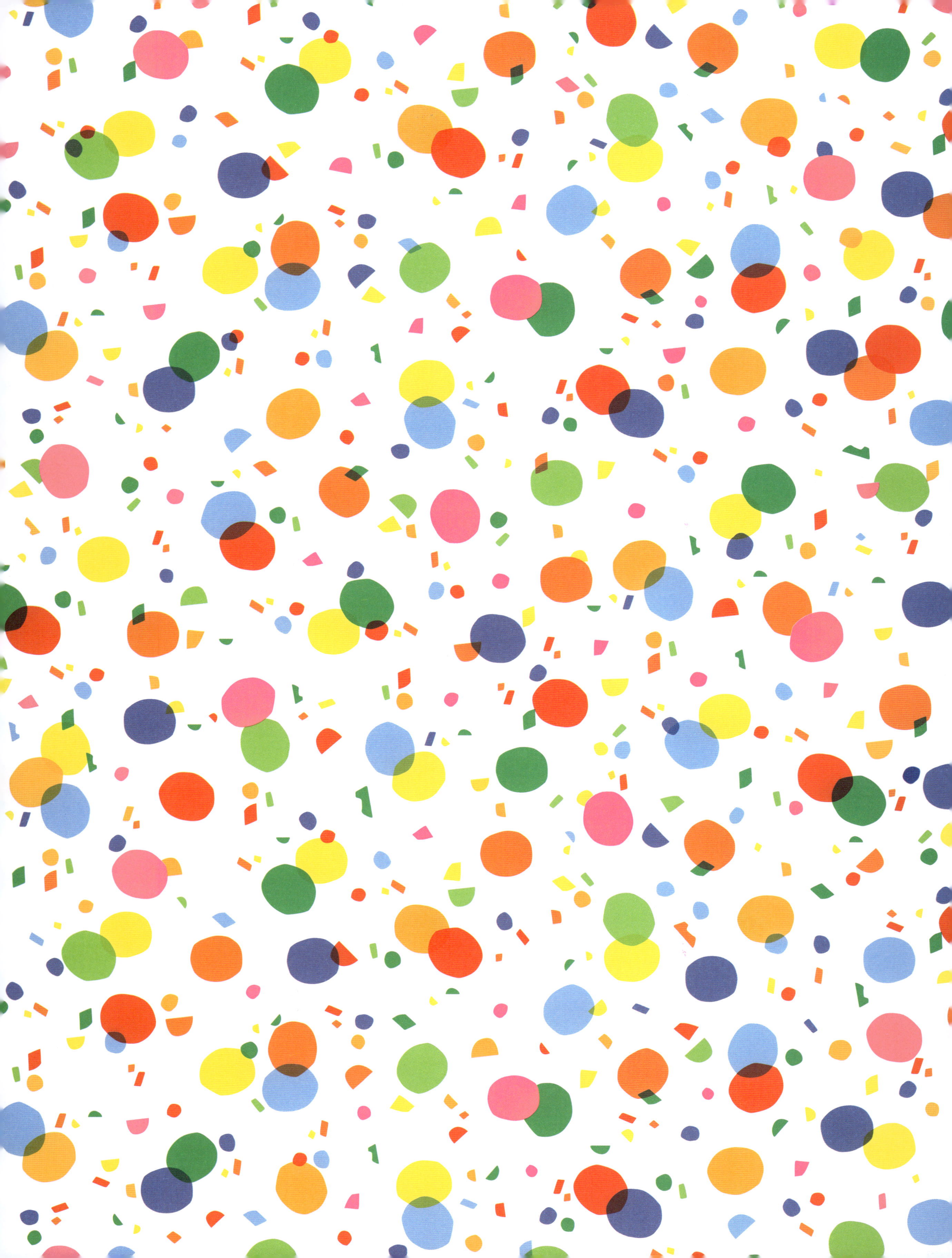

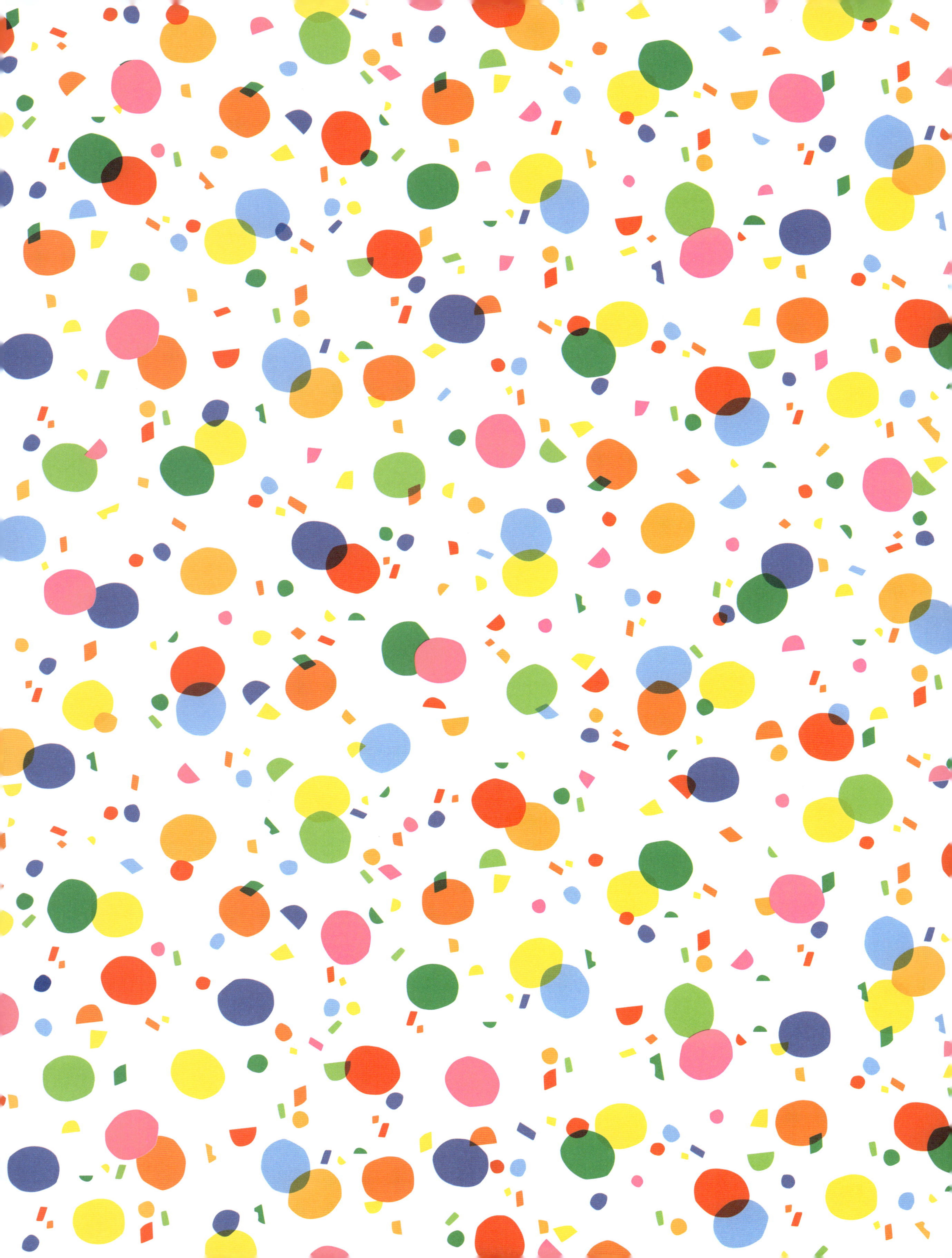

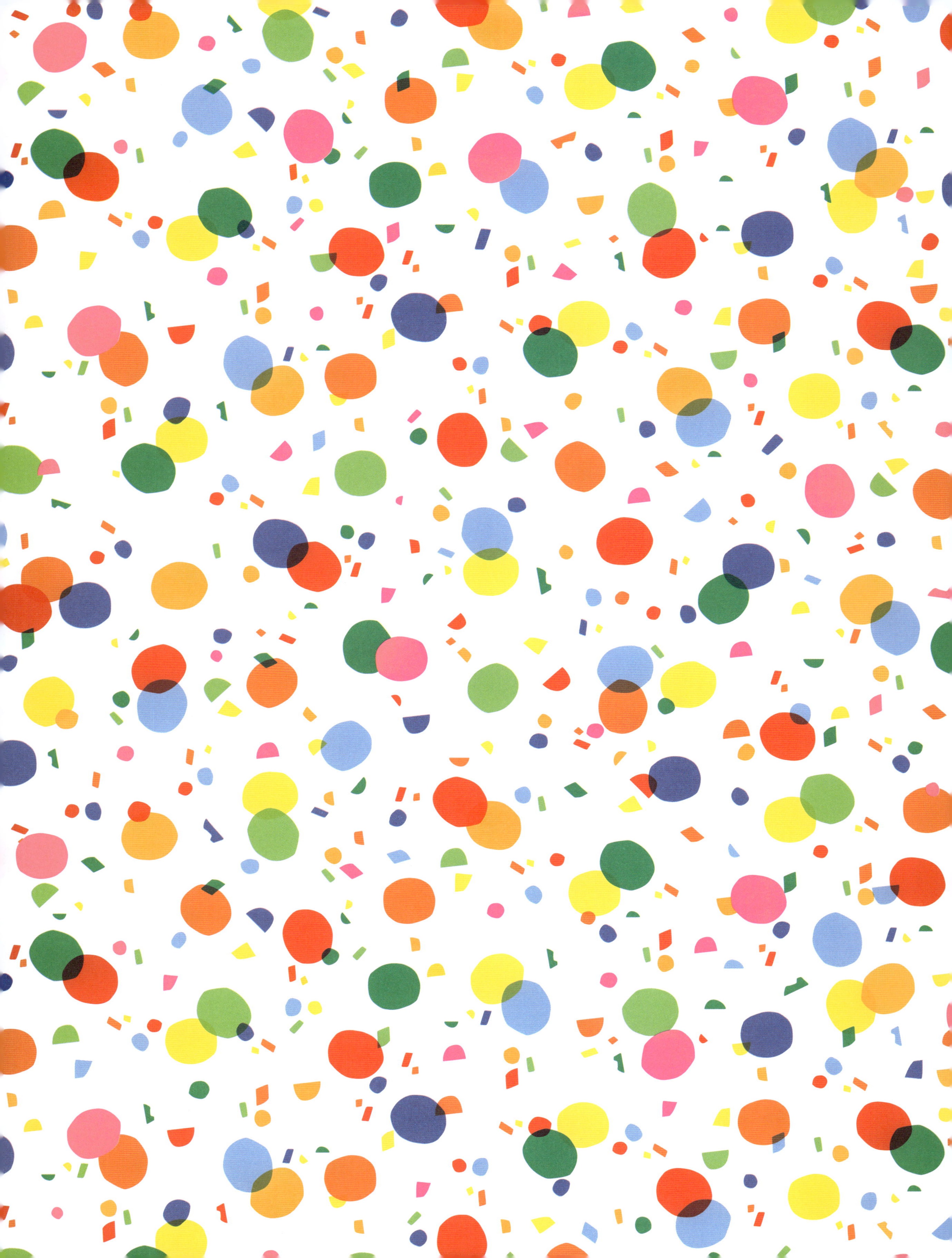

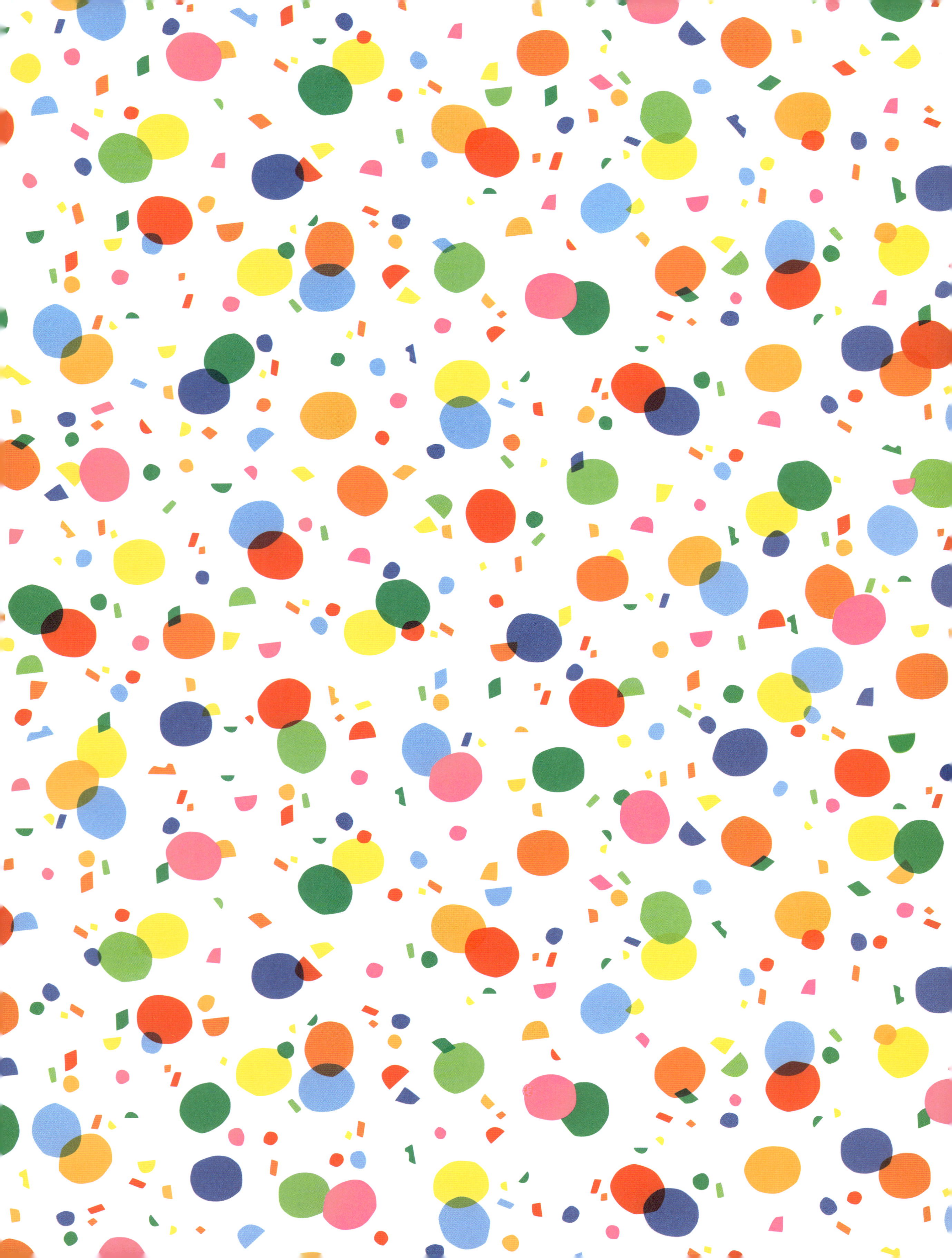

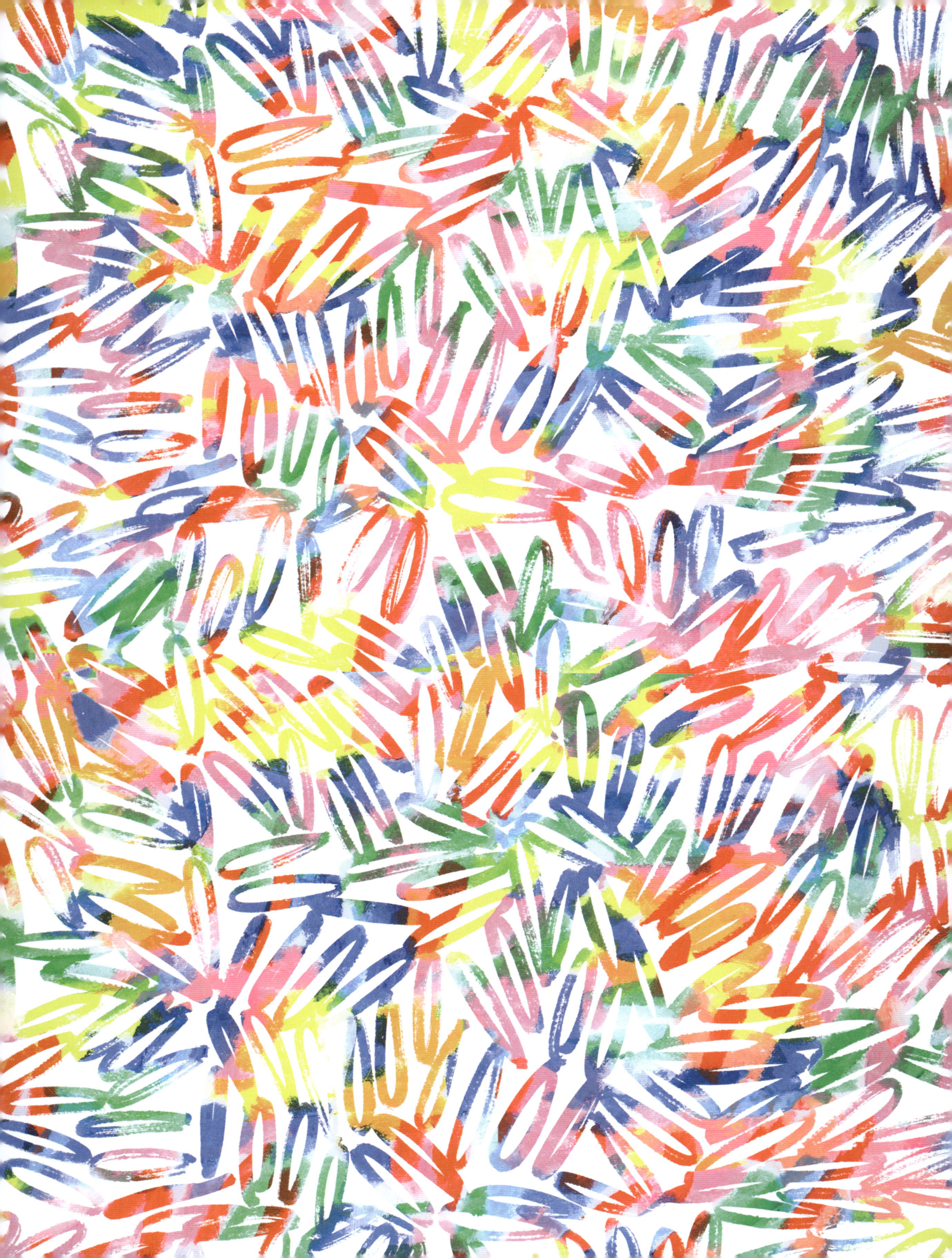

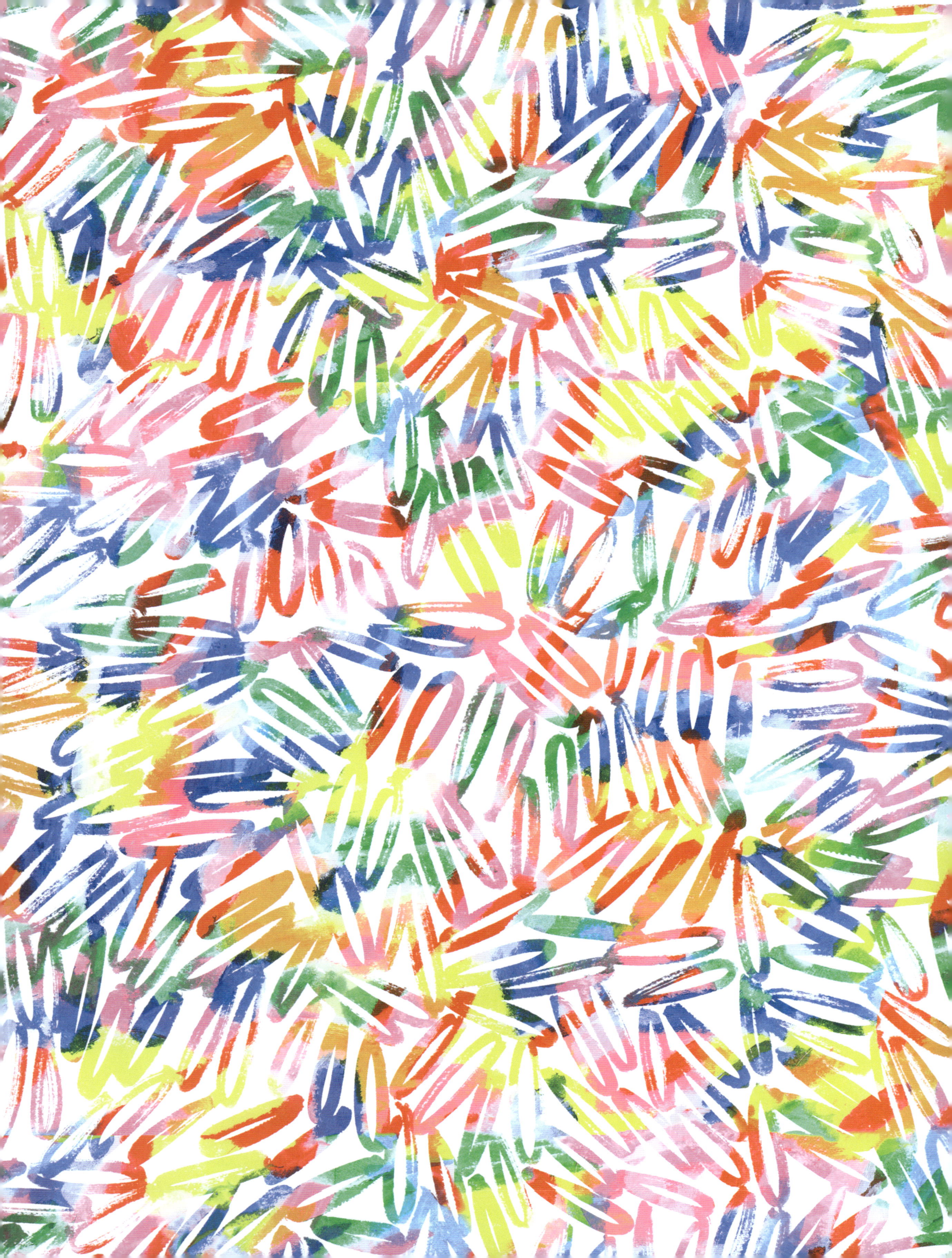

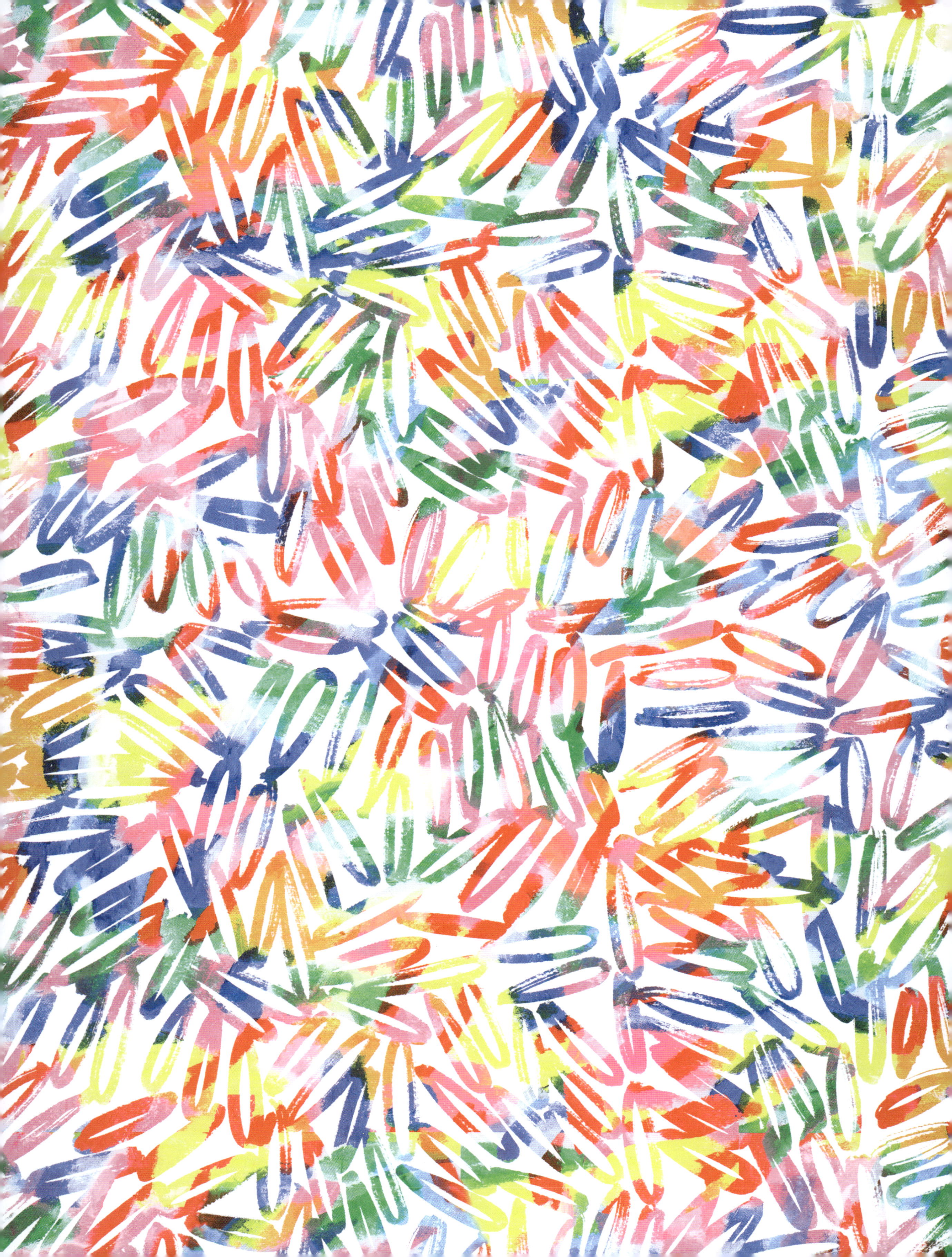

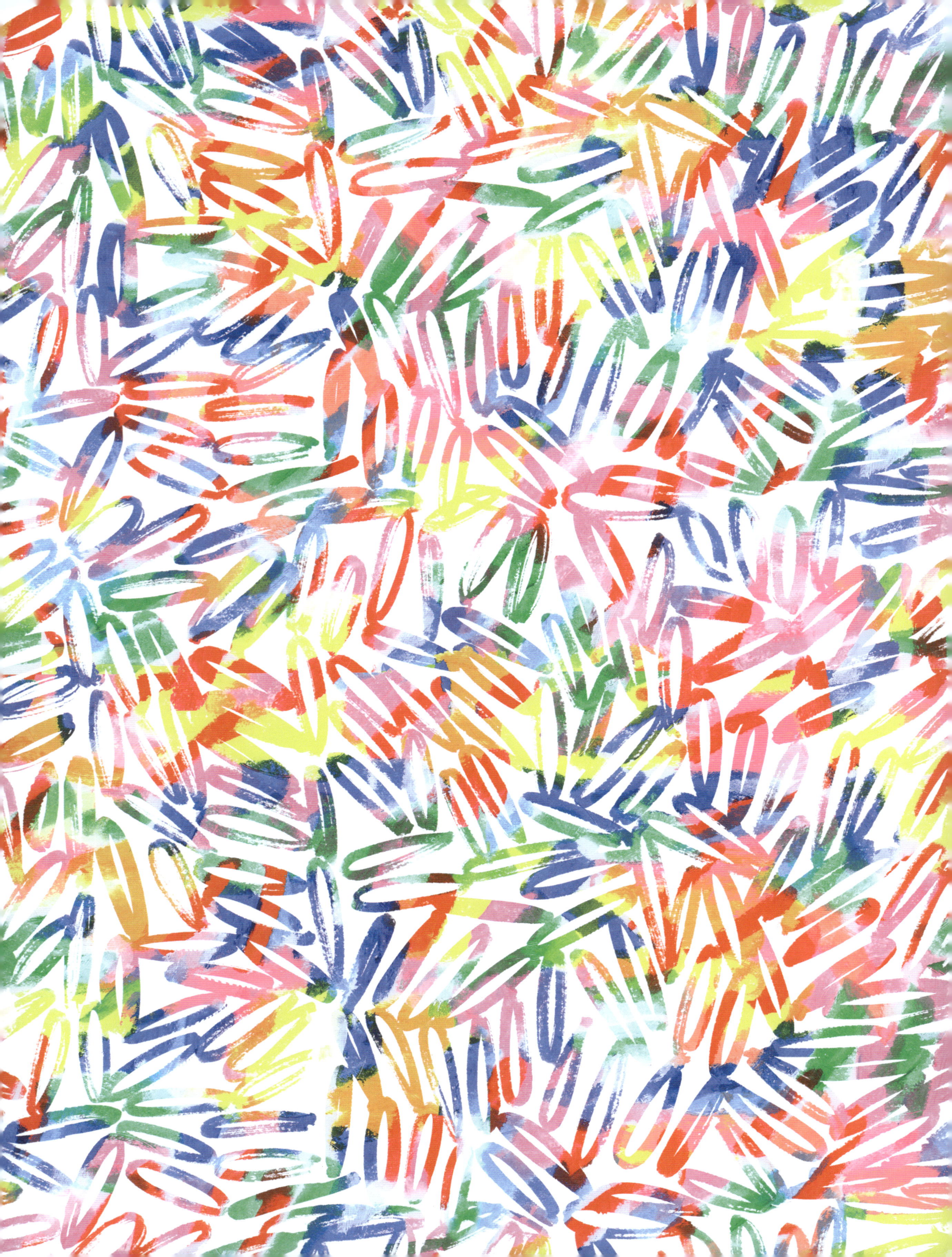

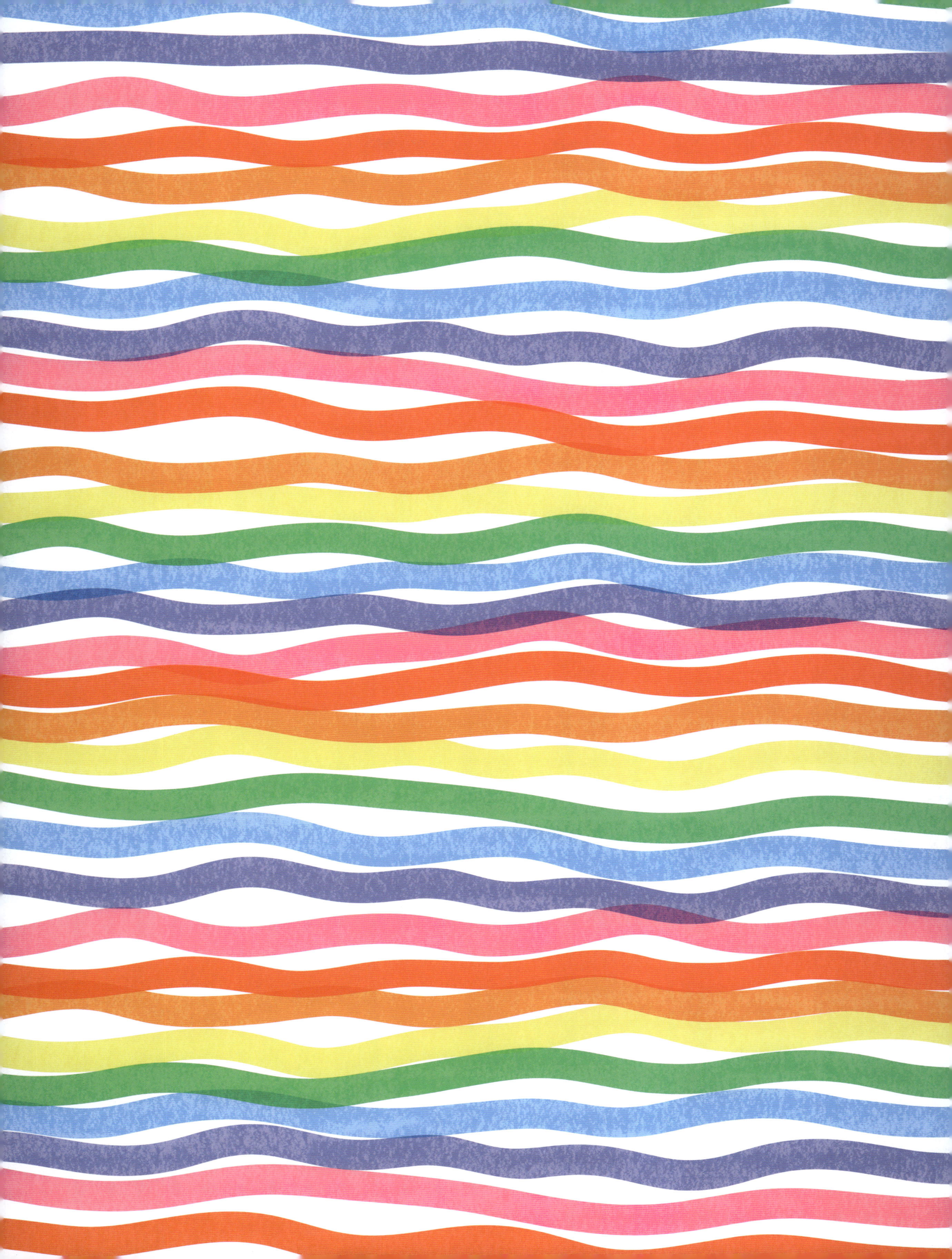

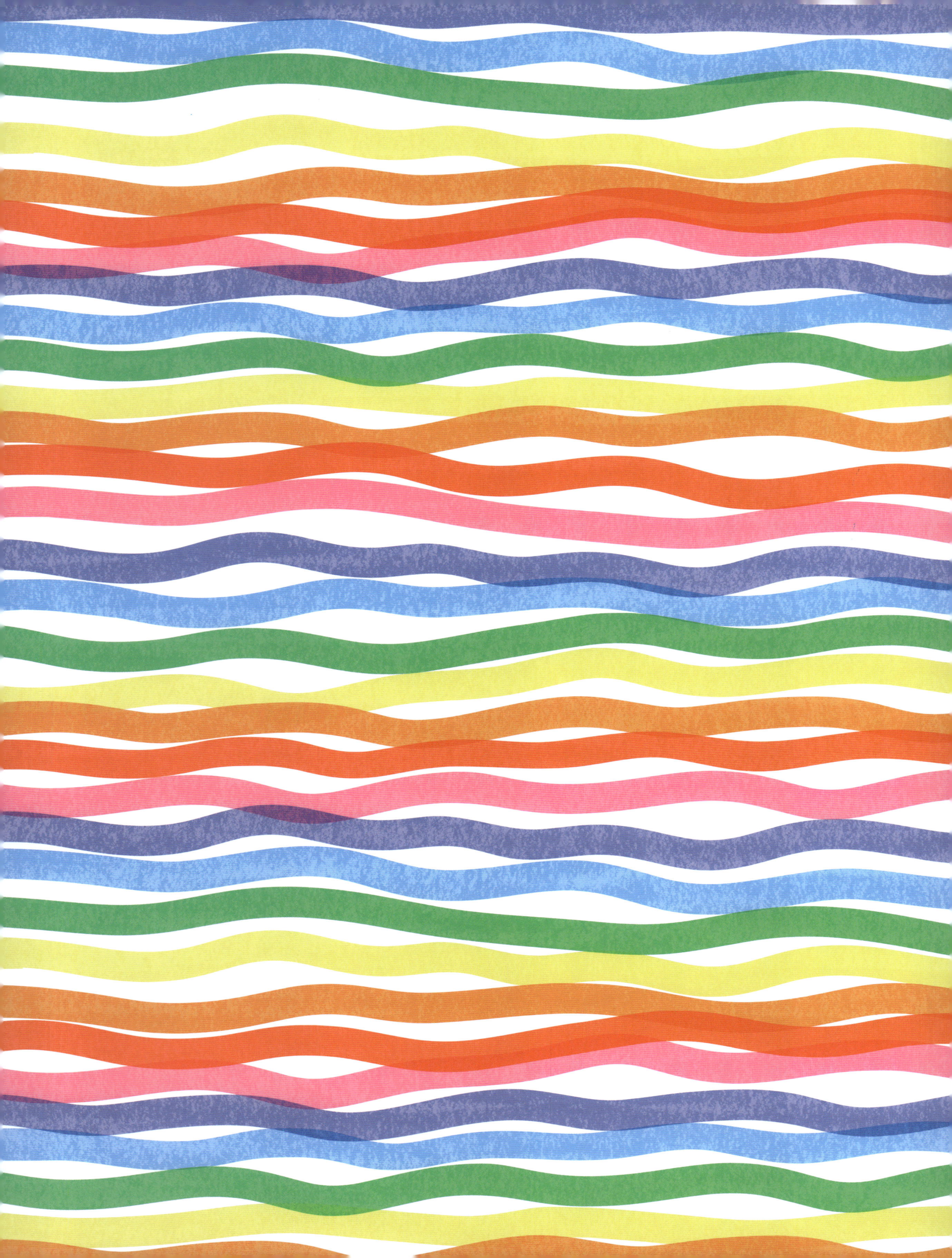

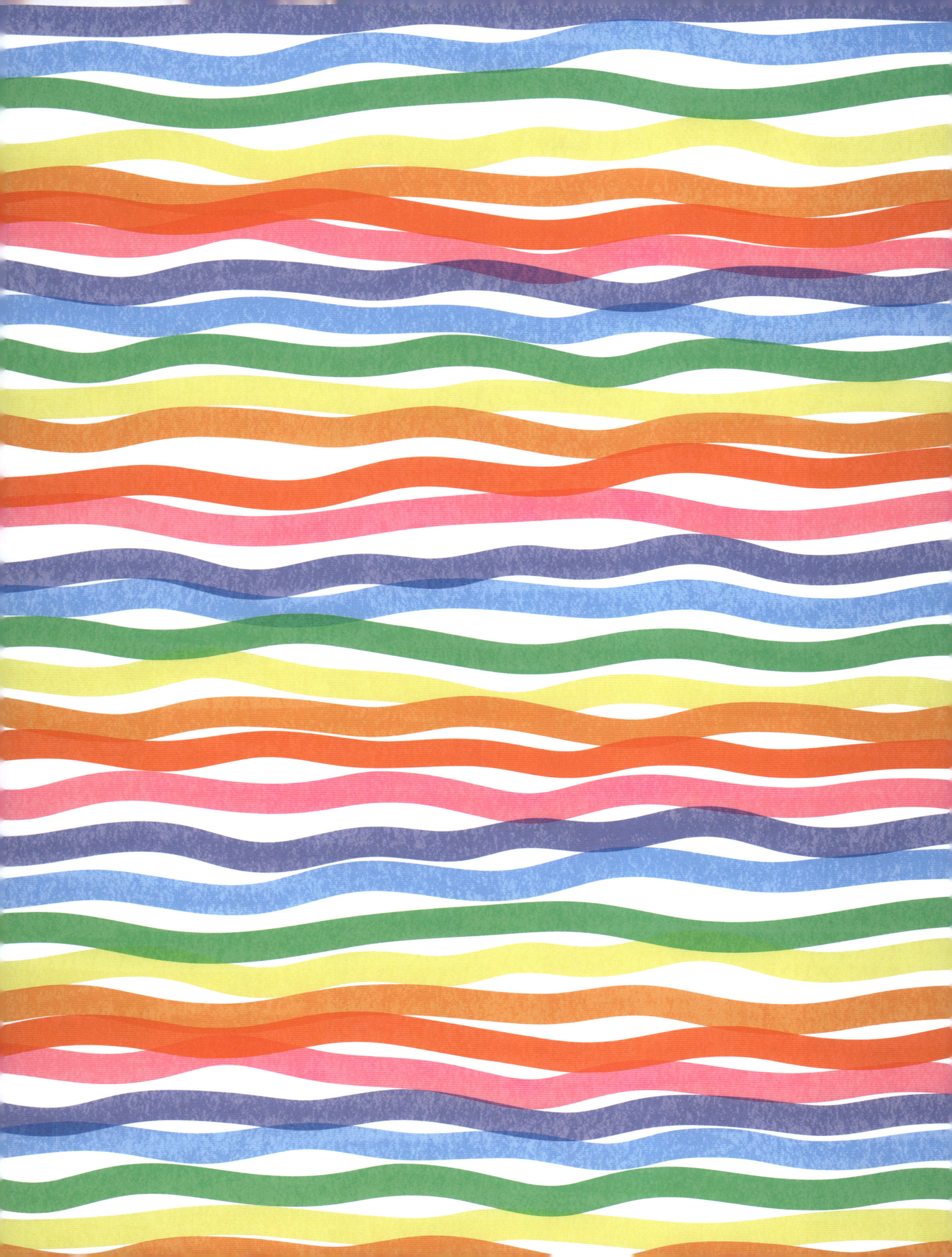

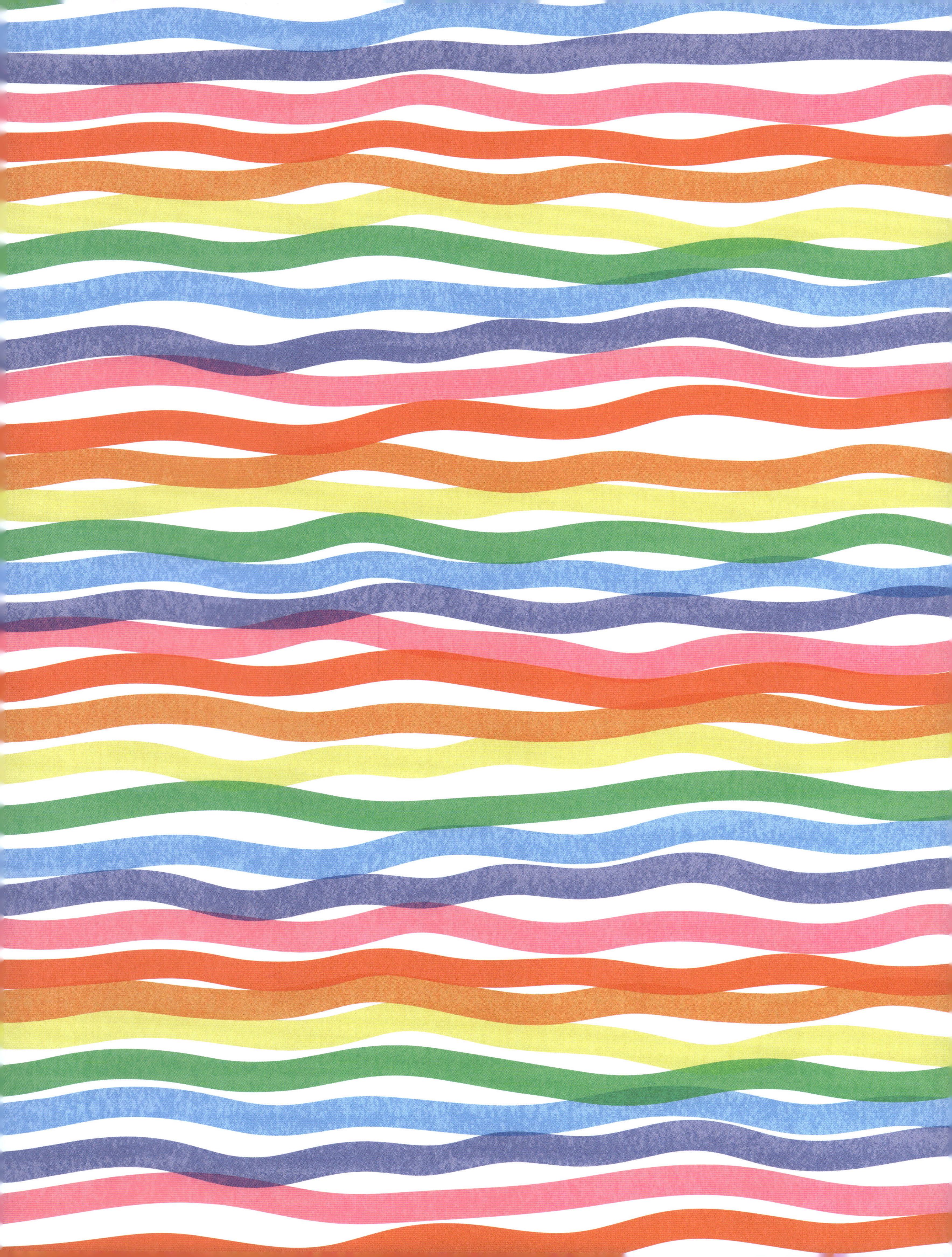

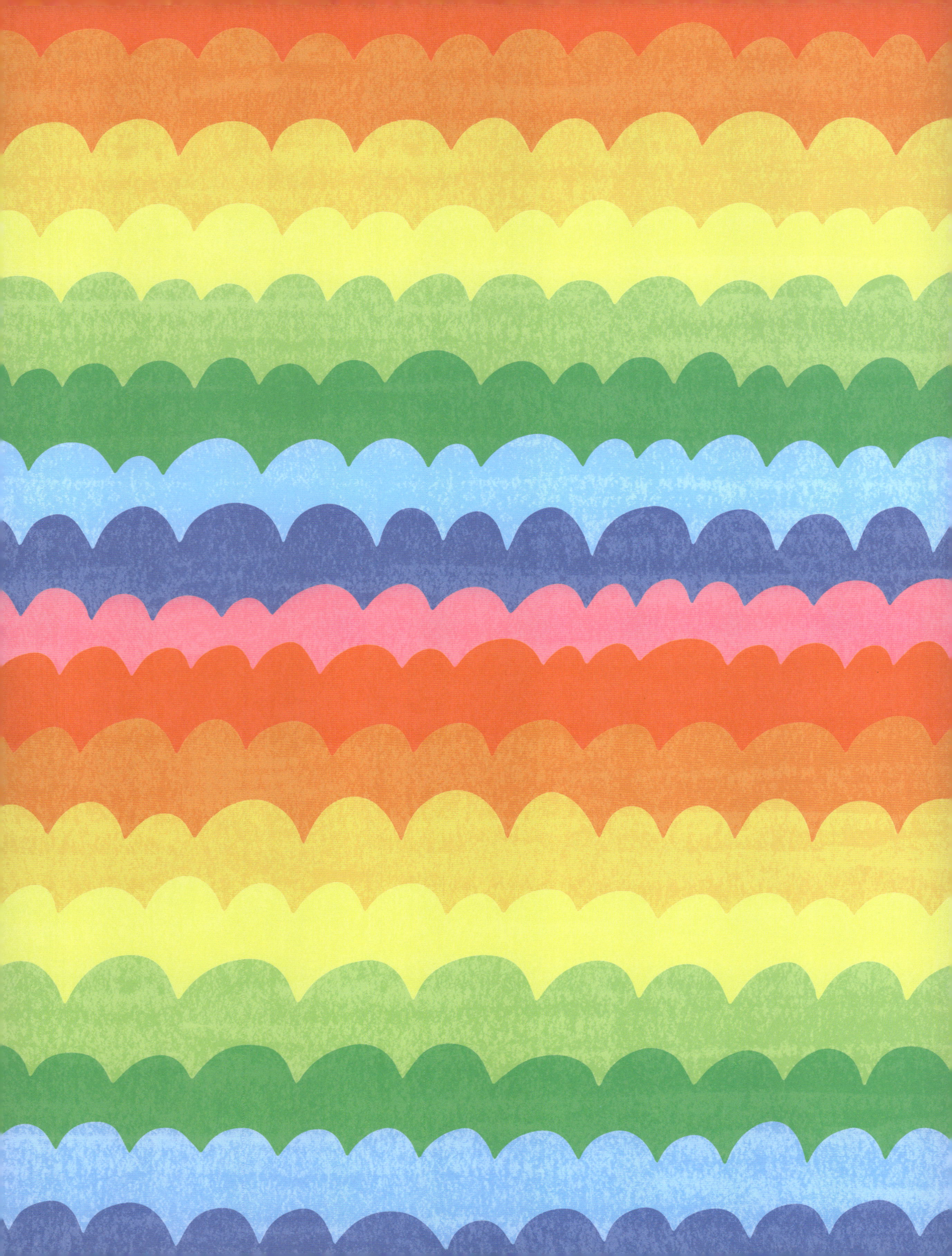

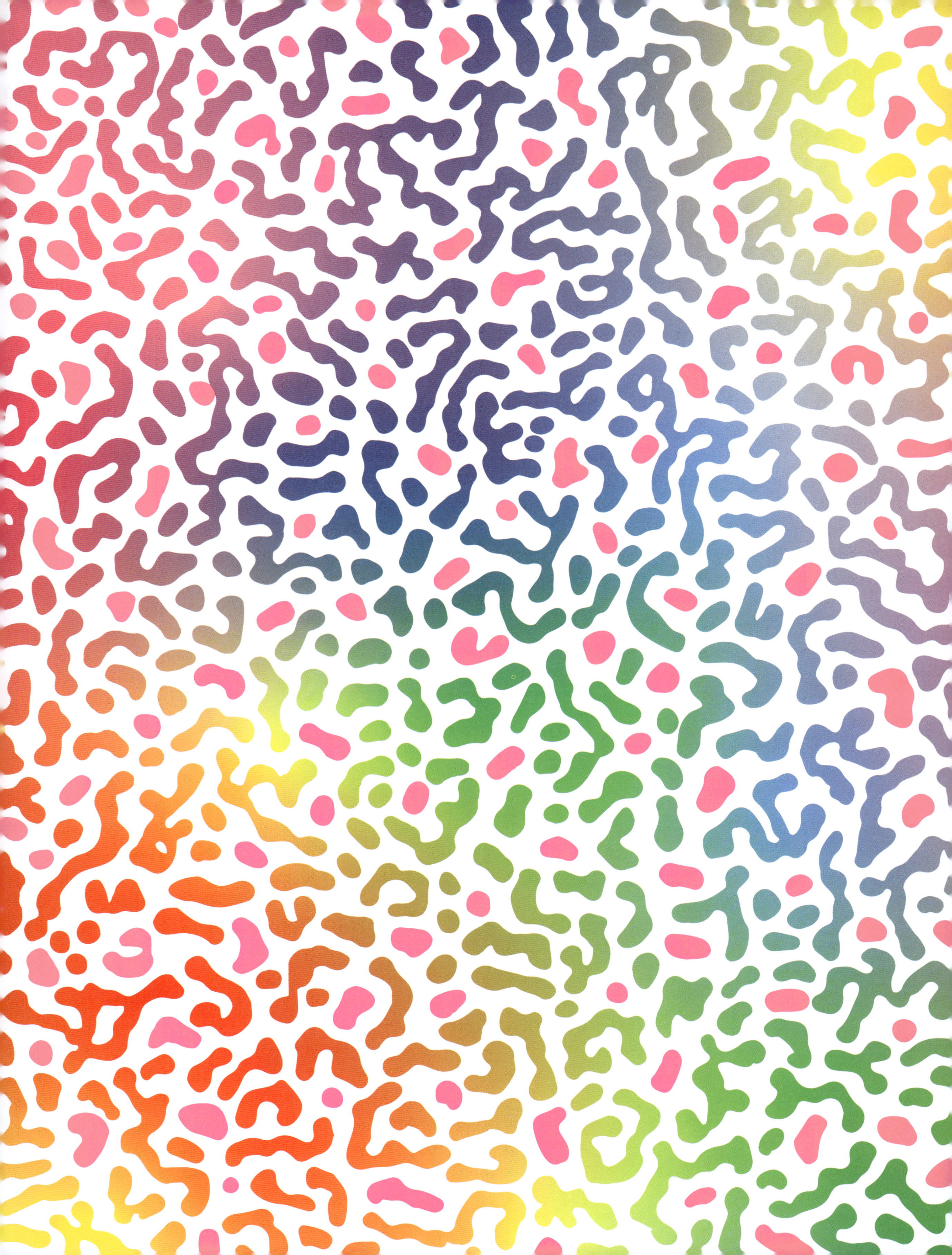

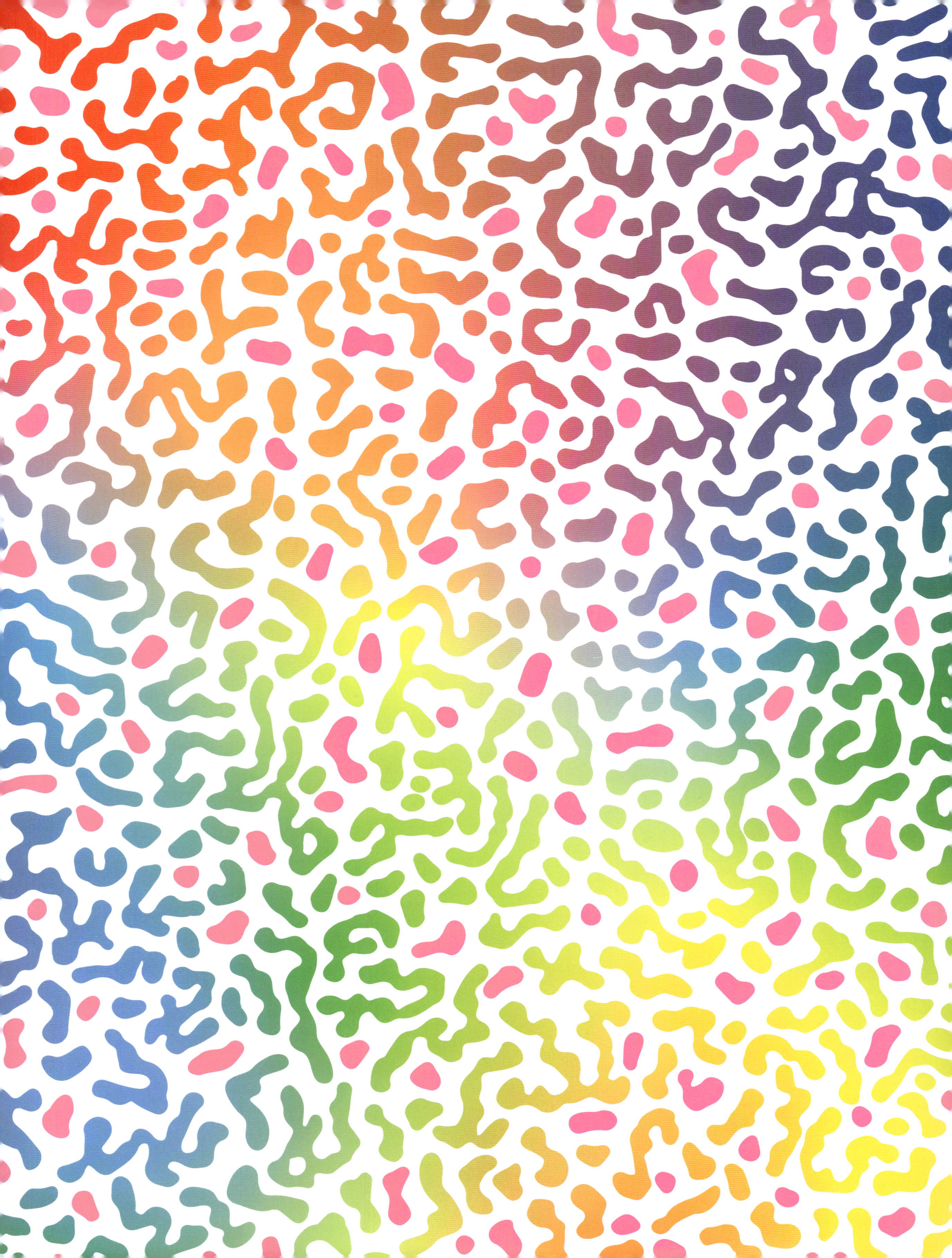

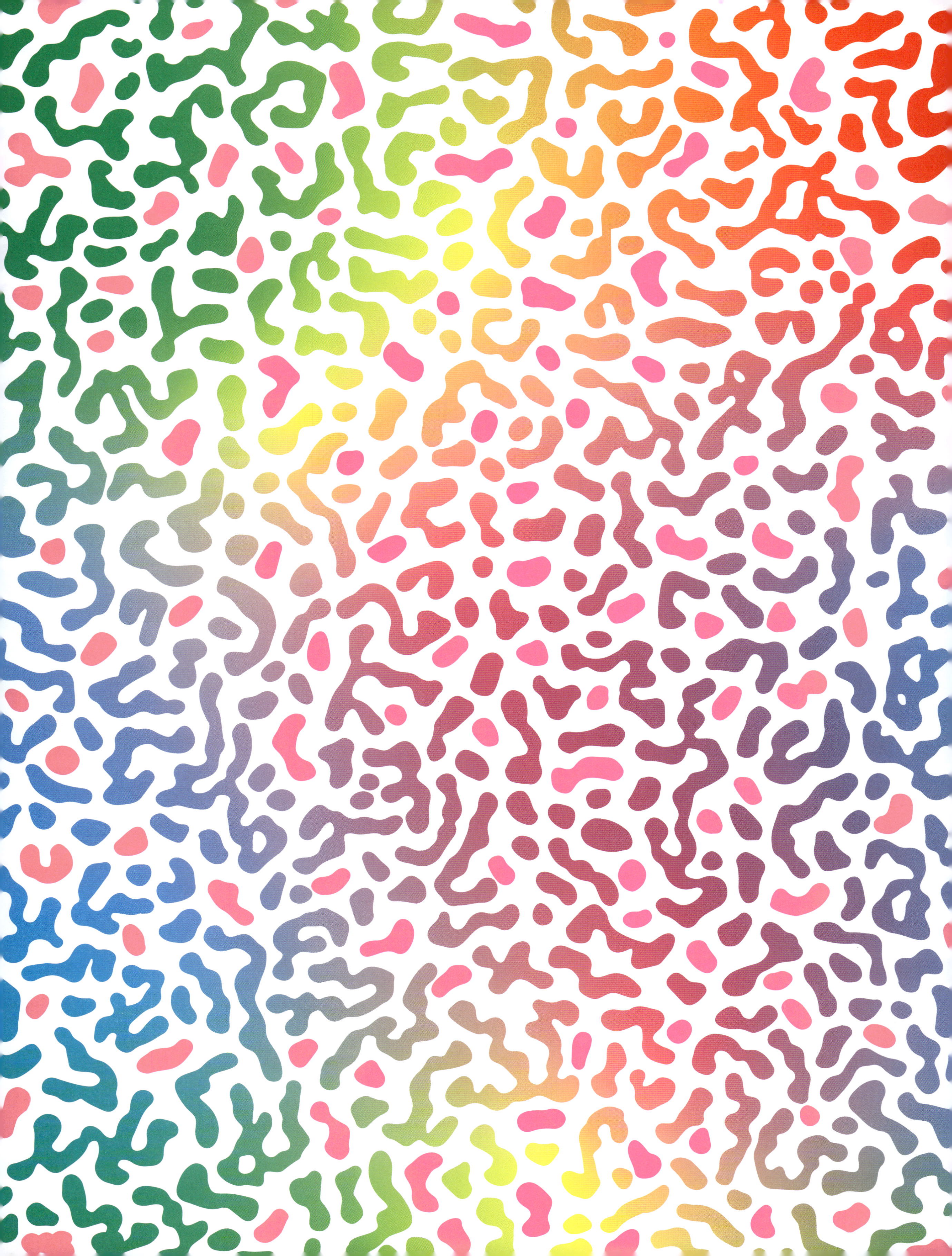

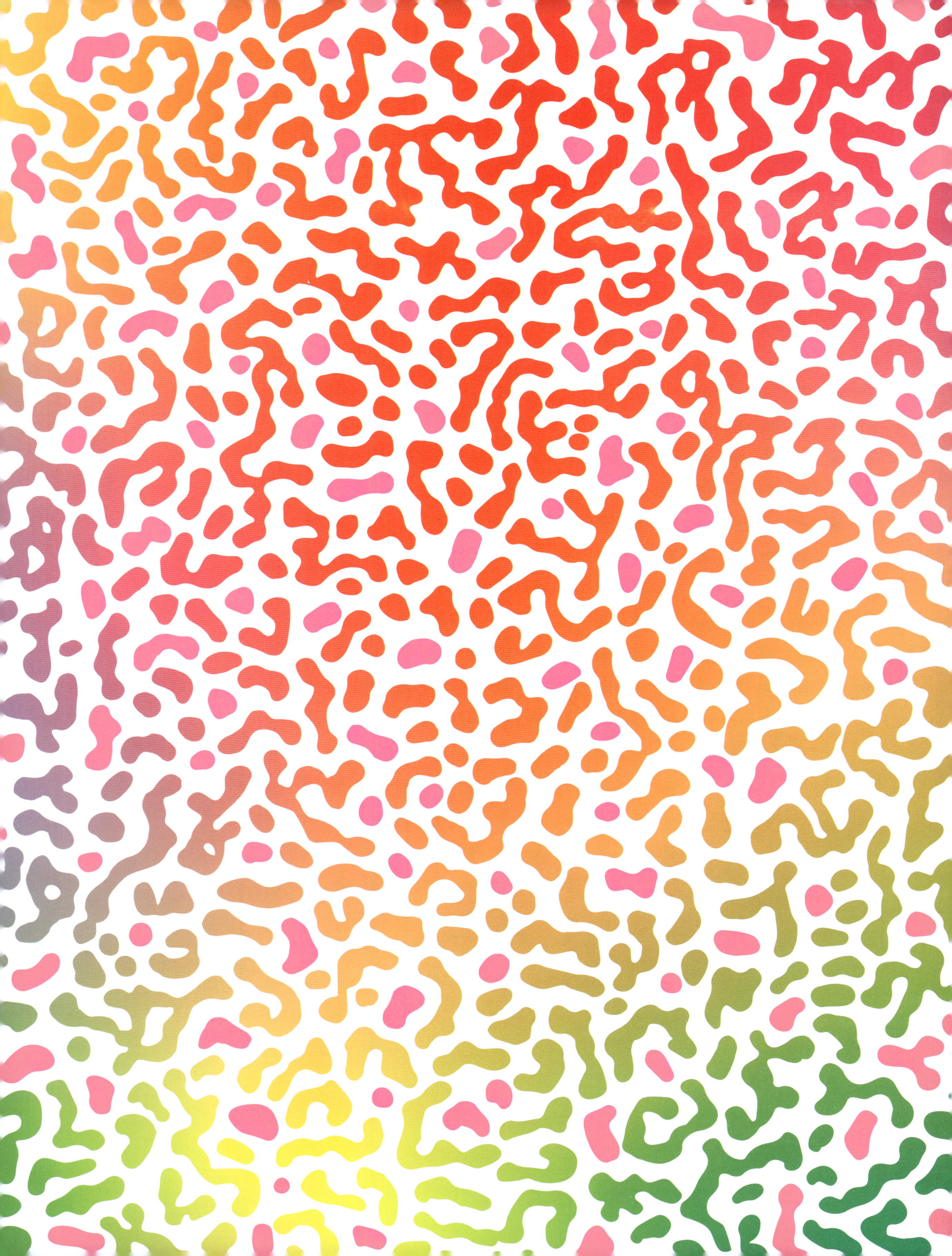

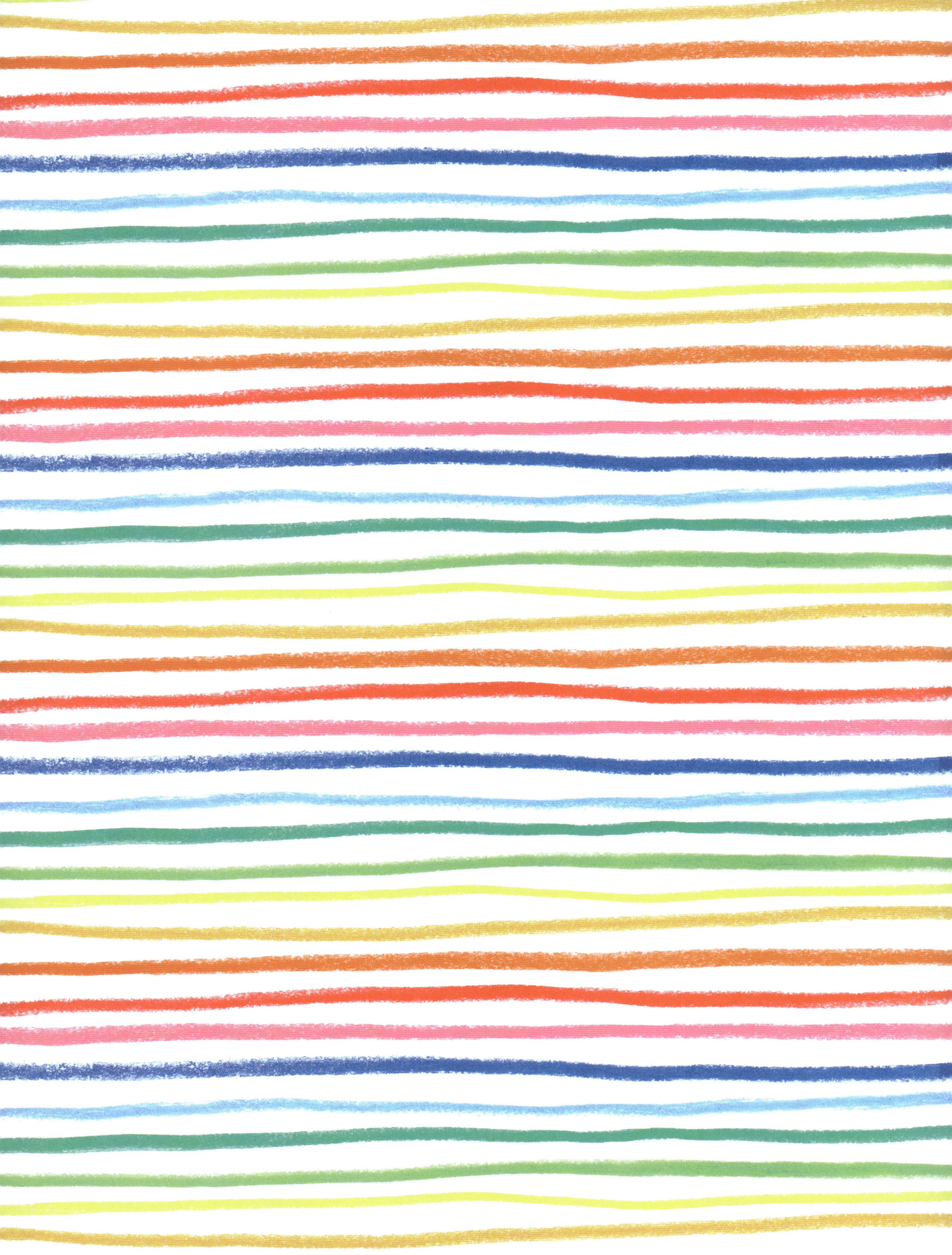

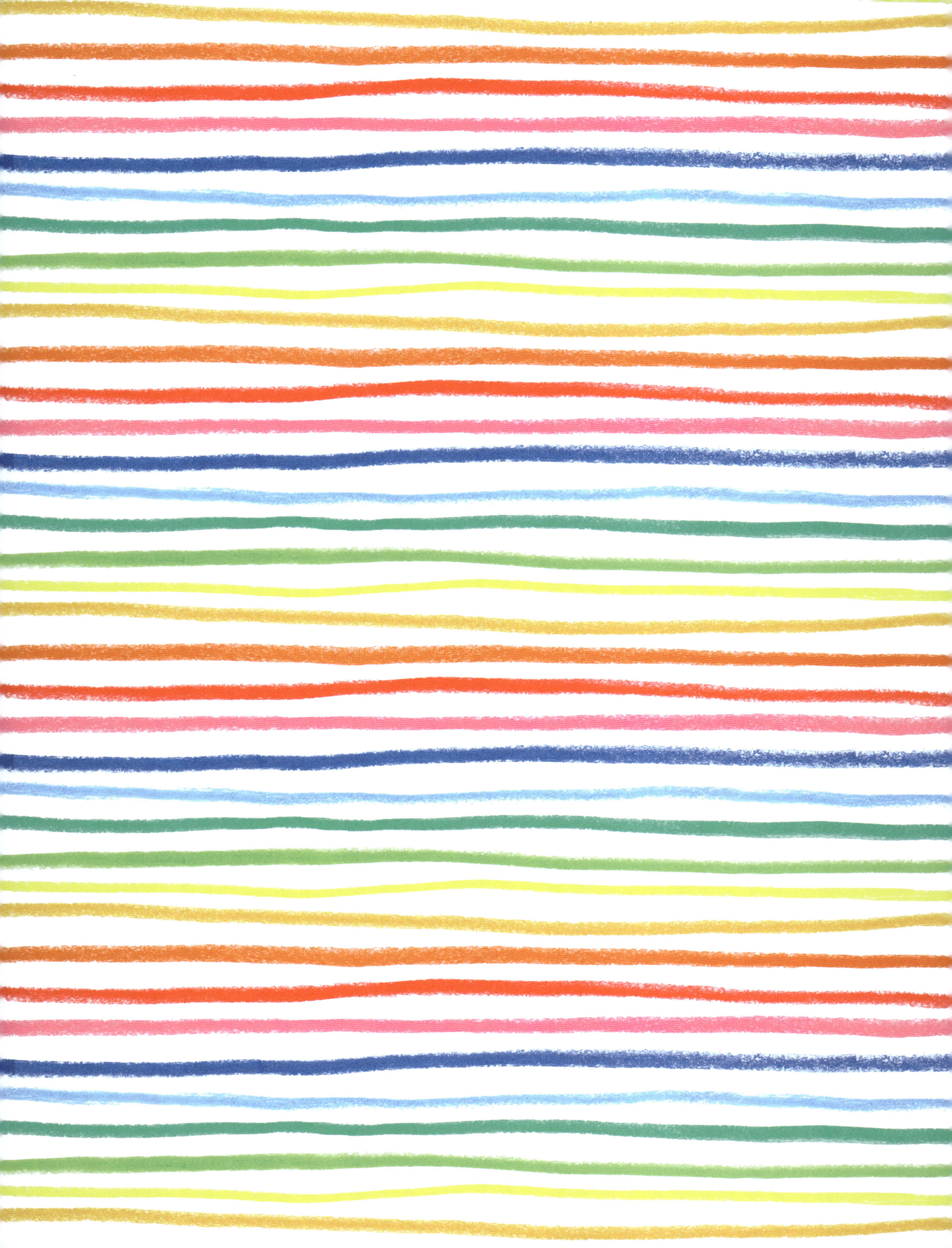

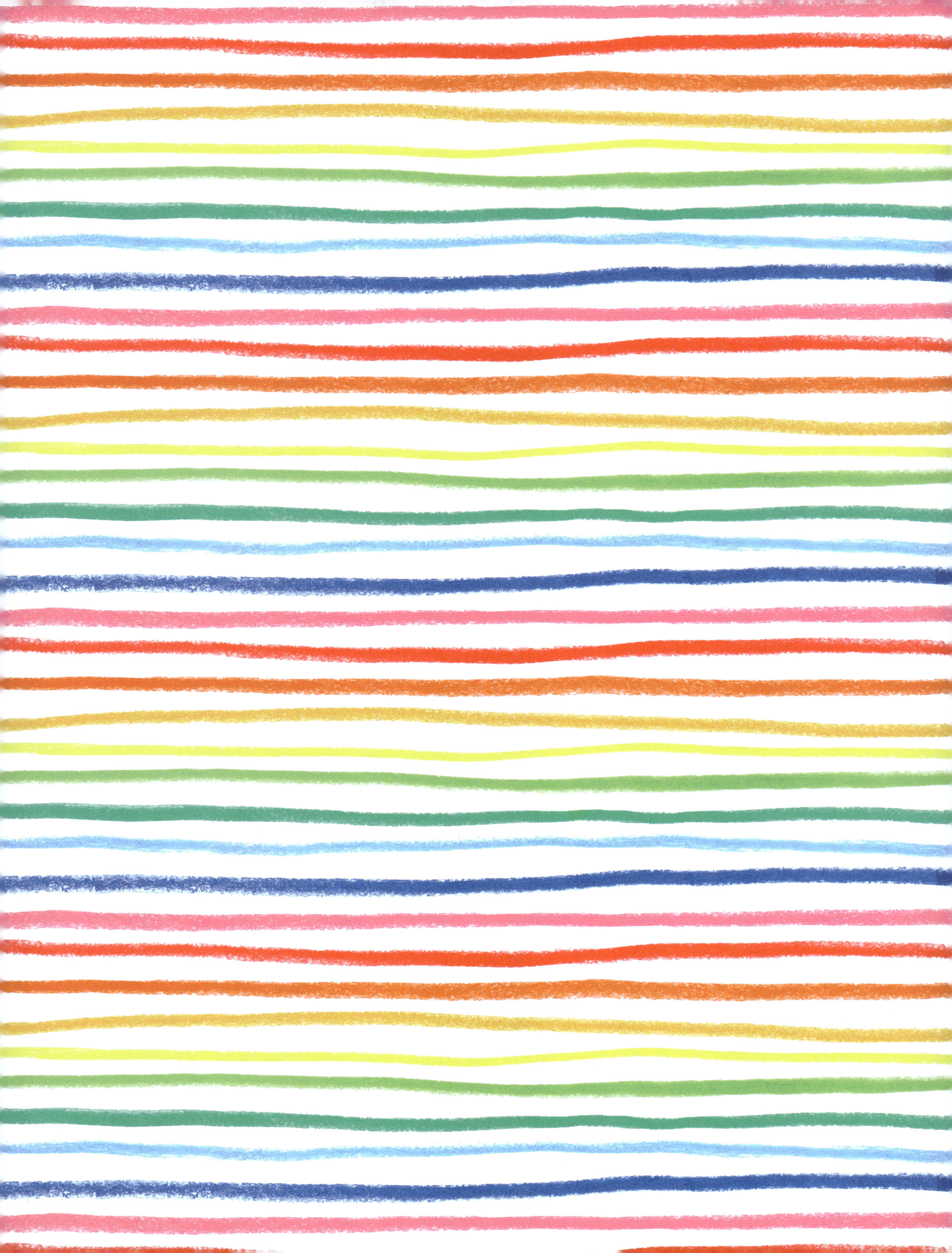

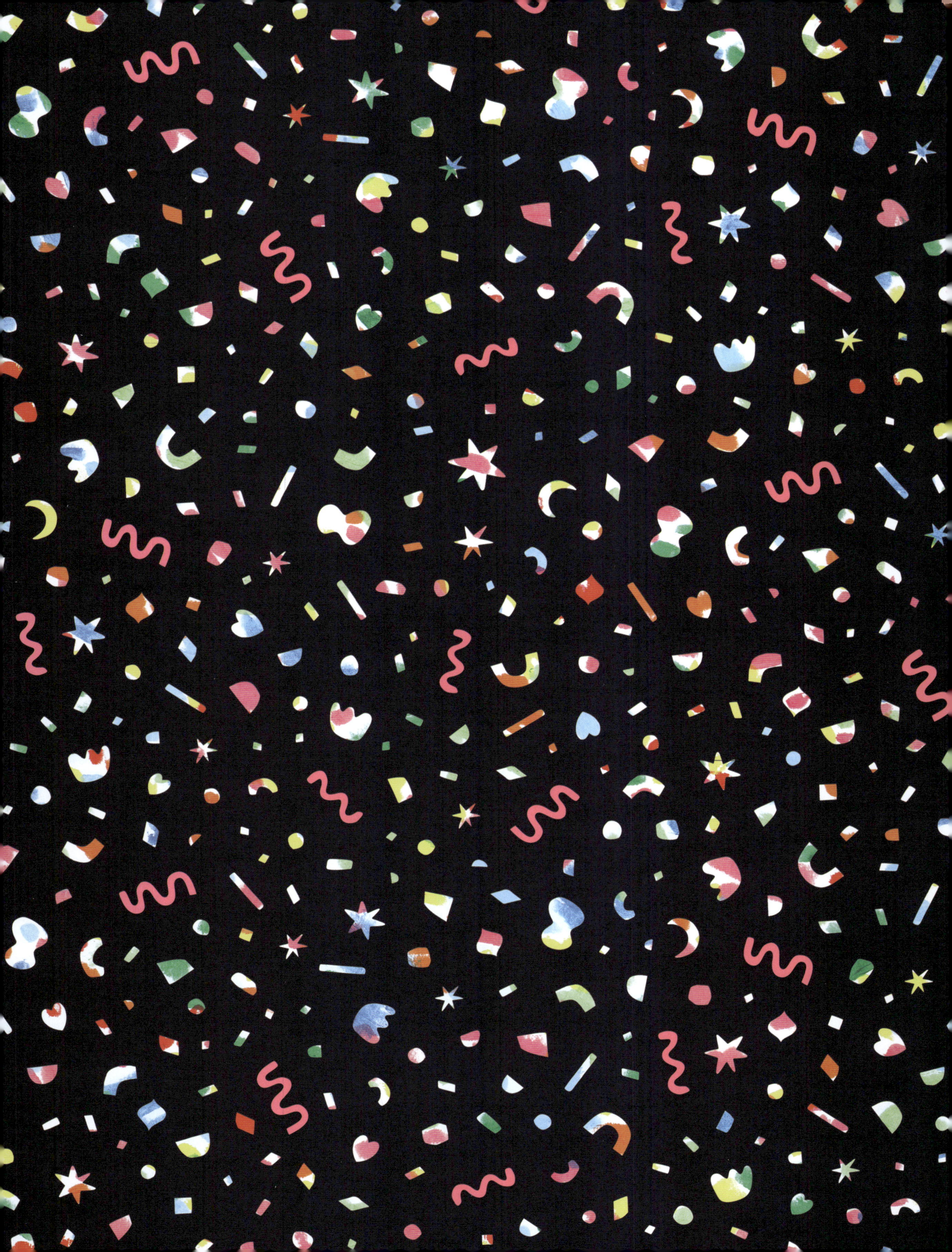

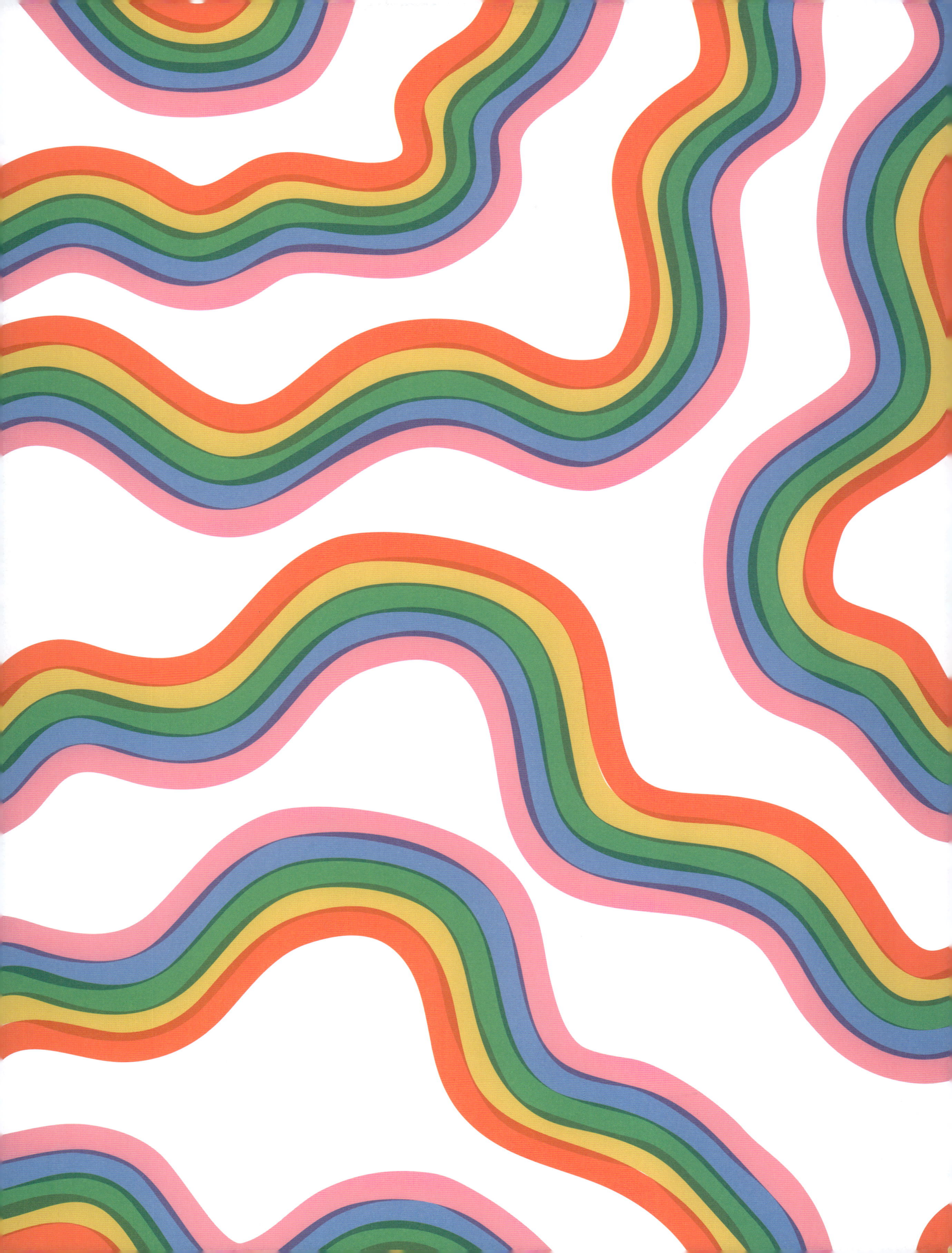

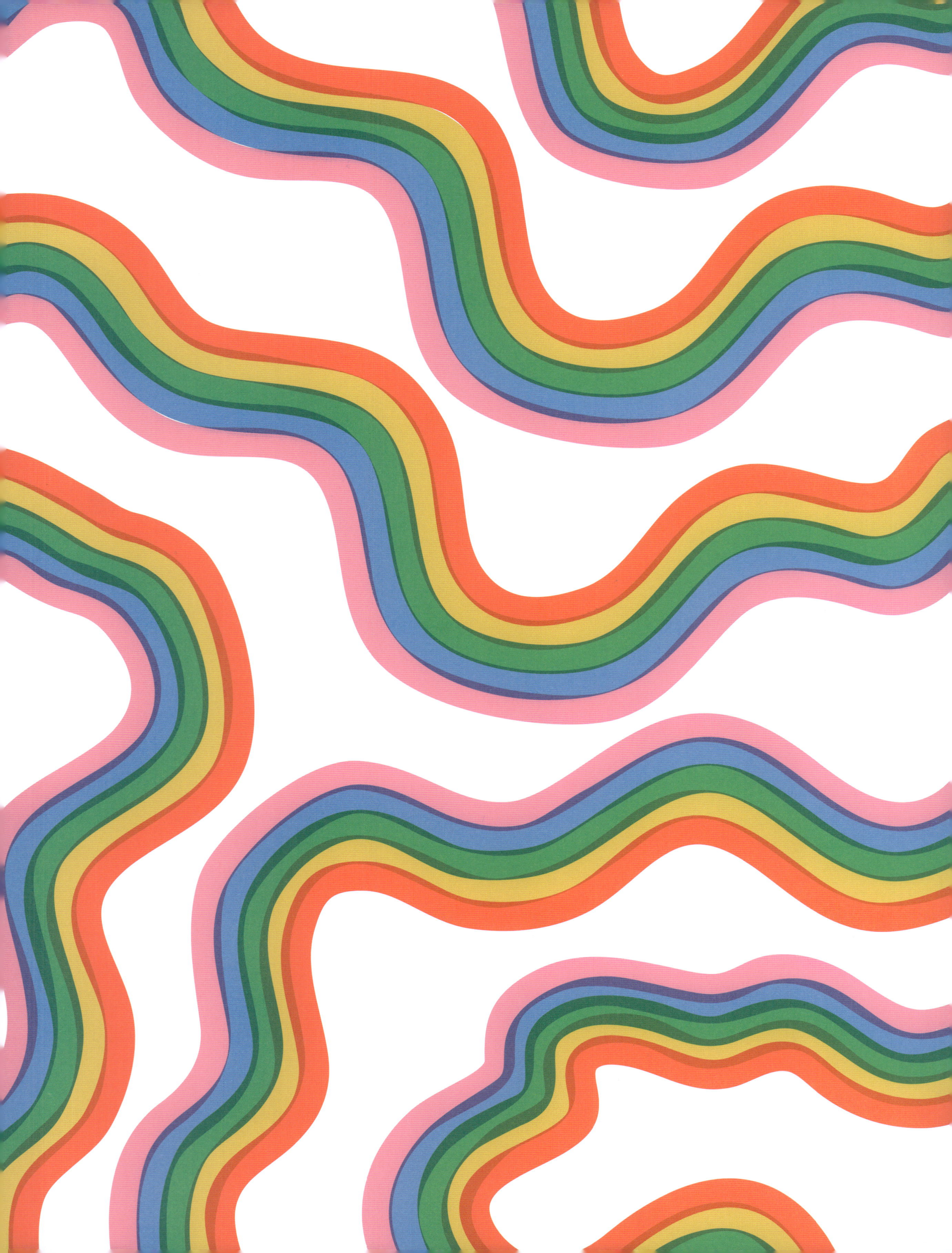

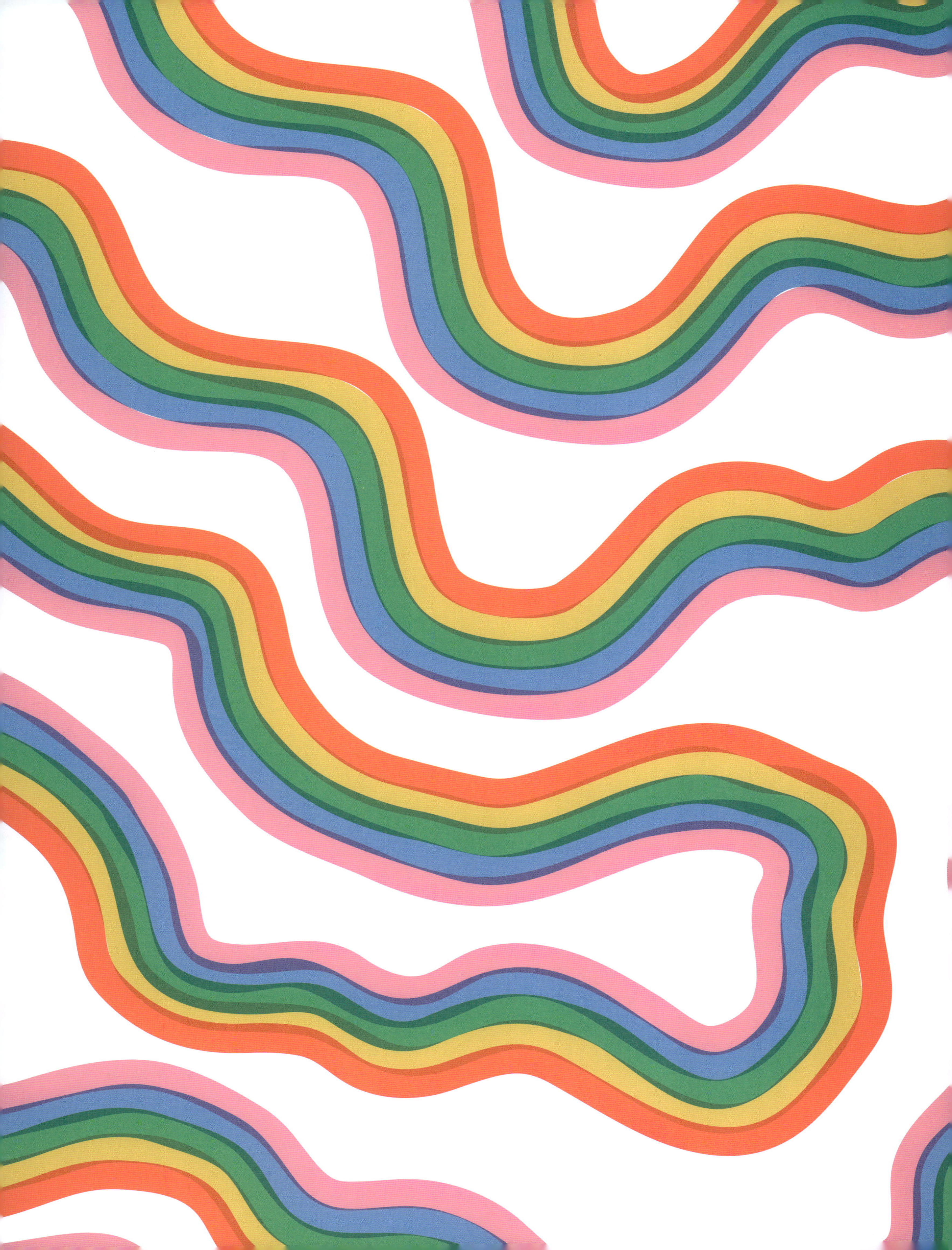

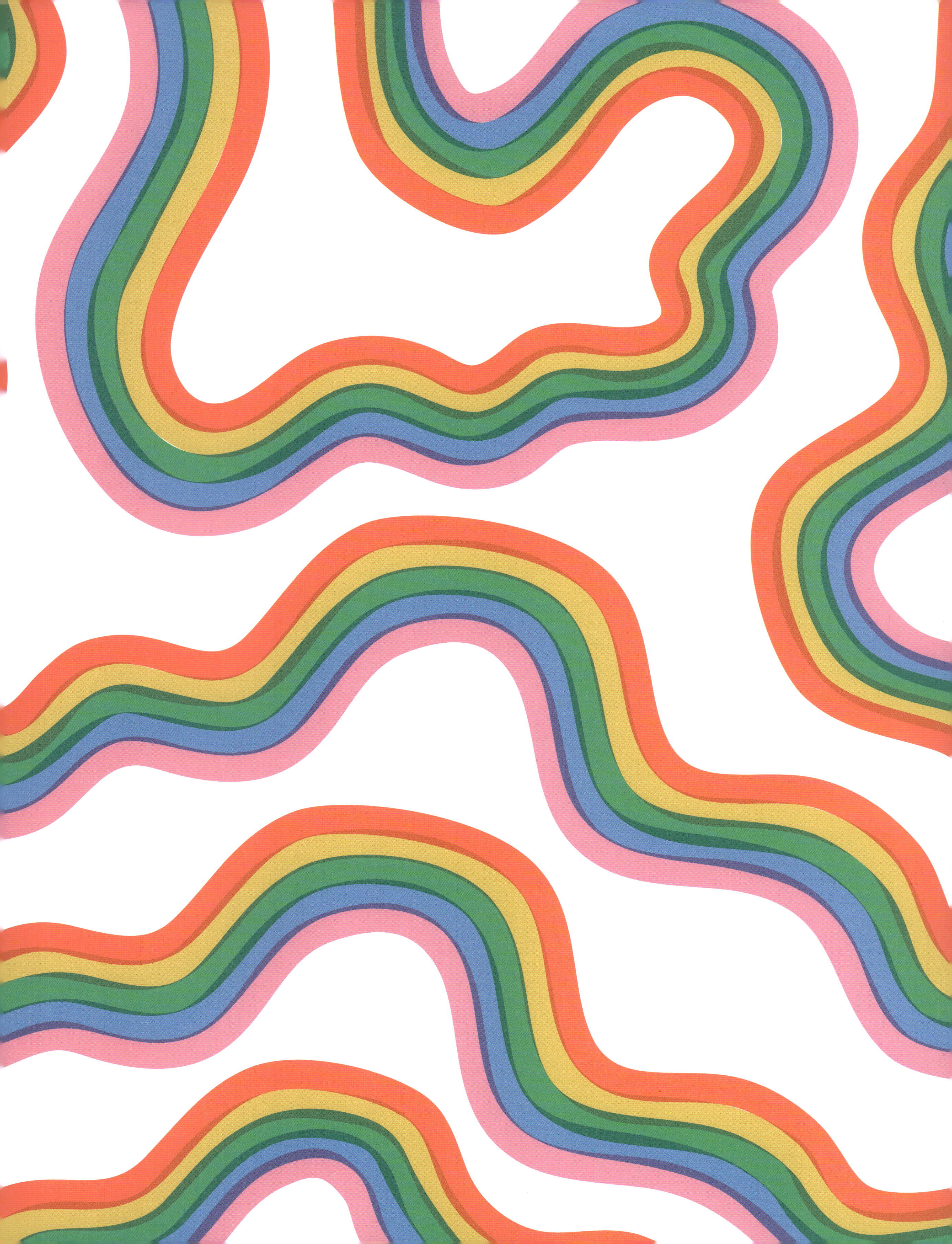

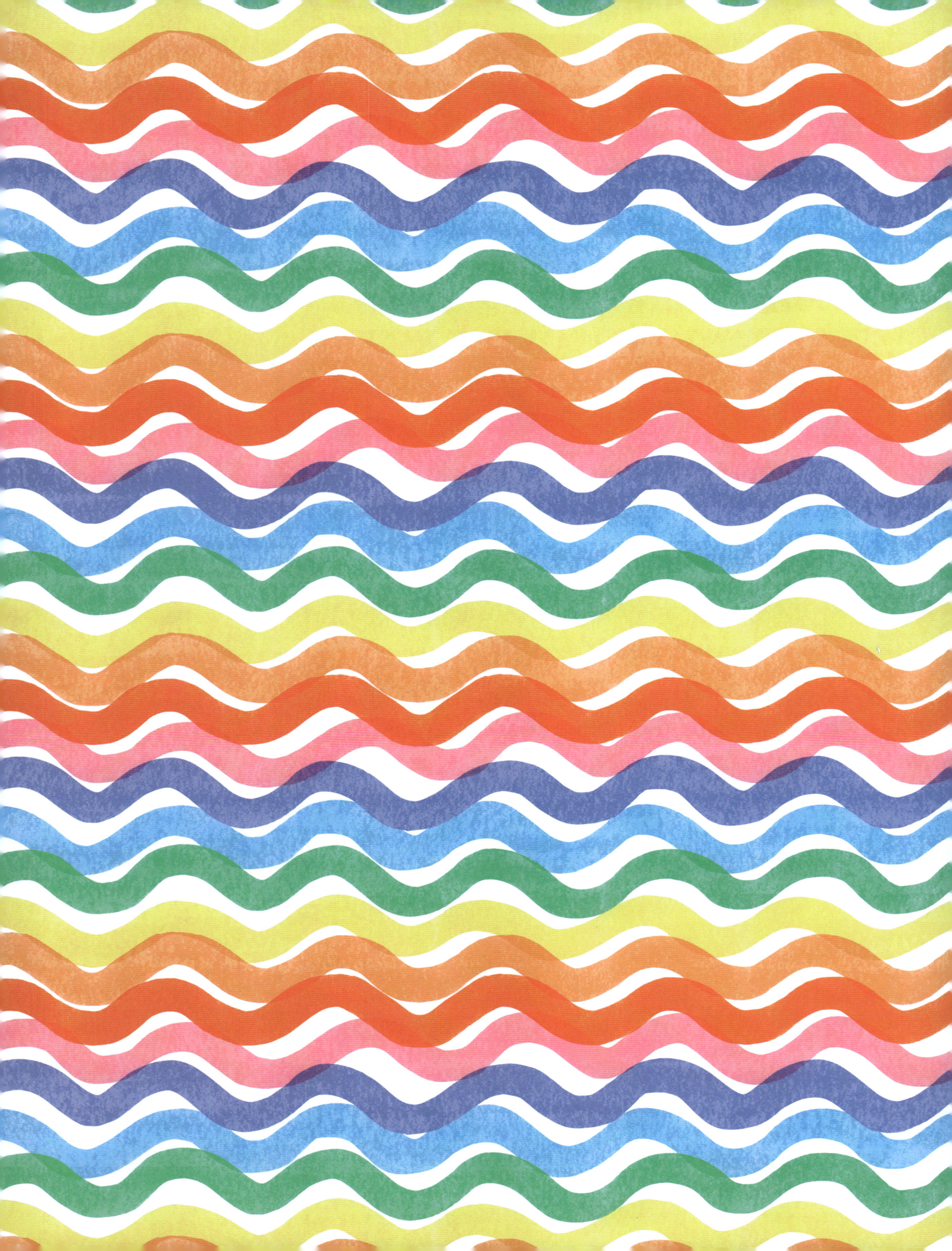

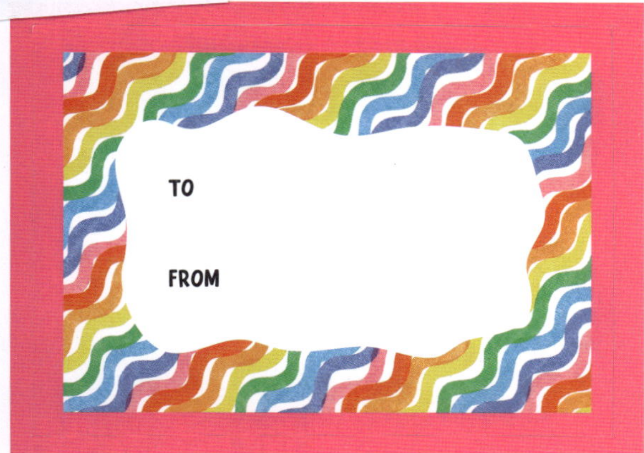
TO
FROM
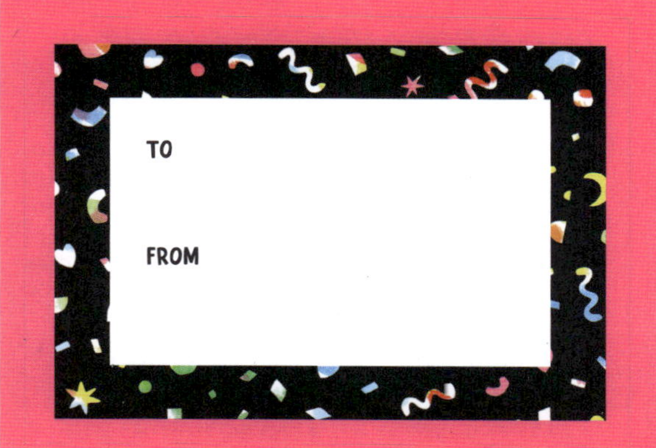
TO
FROM
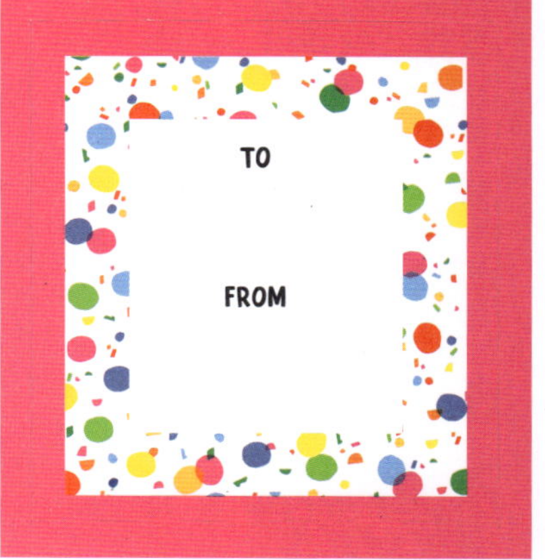
TO
FROM
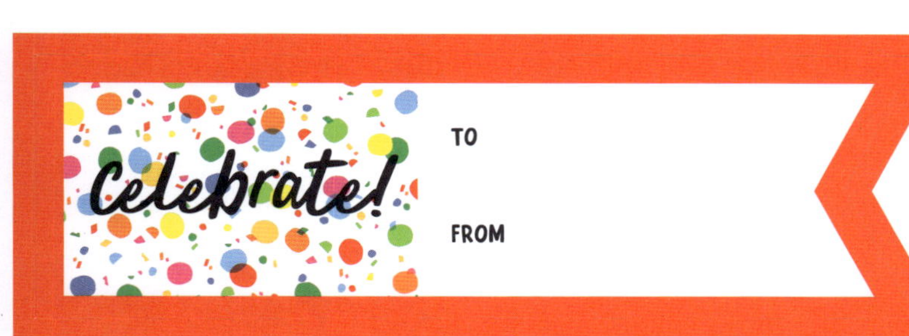
Celebrate!
TO
FROM
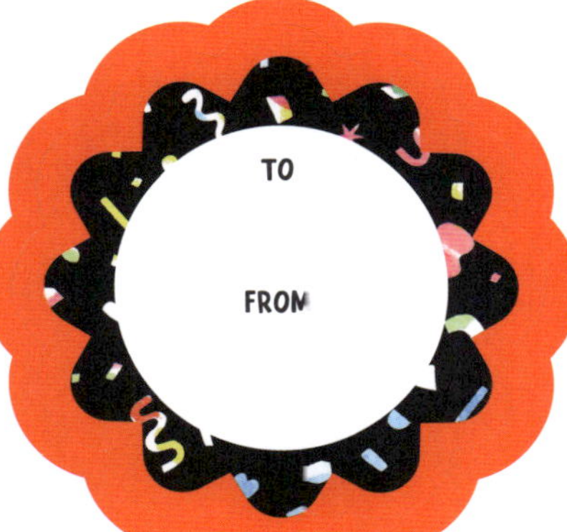
TO
FROM
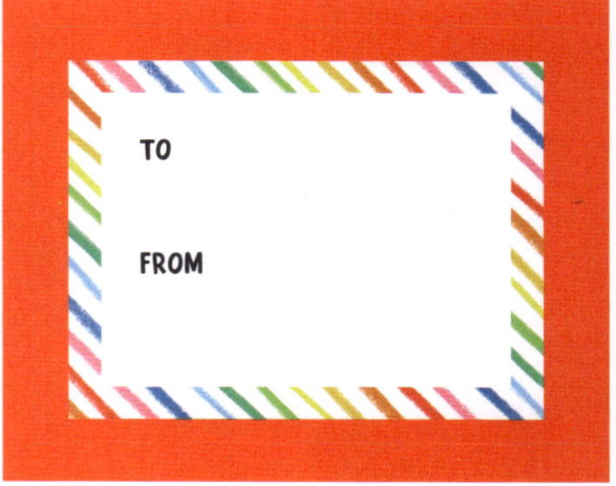
TO
FROM
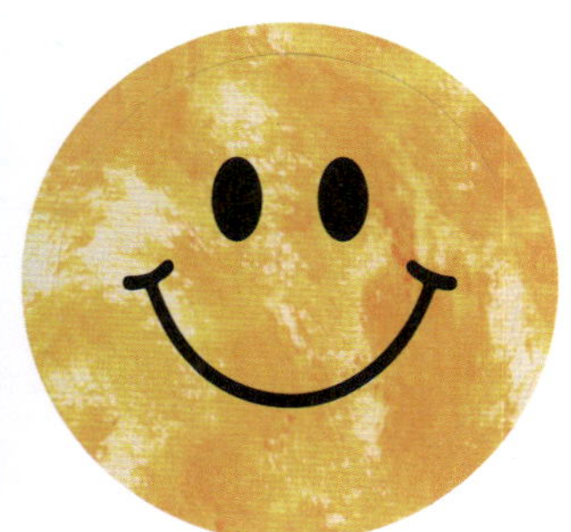
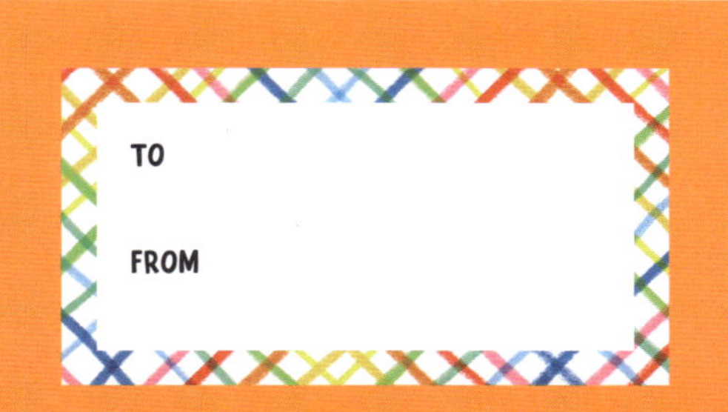
TO
FROM
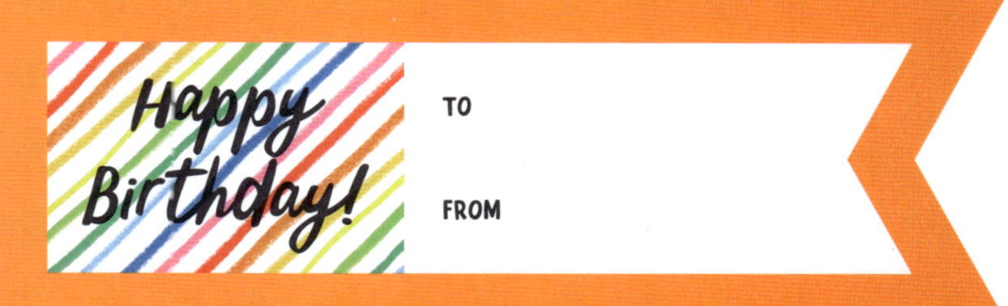
Happy Birthday!
TO
FROM

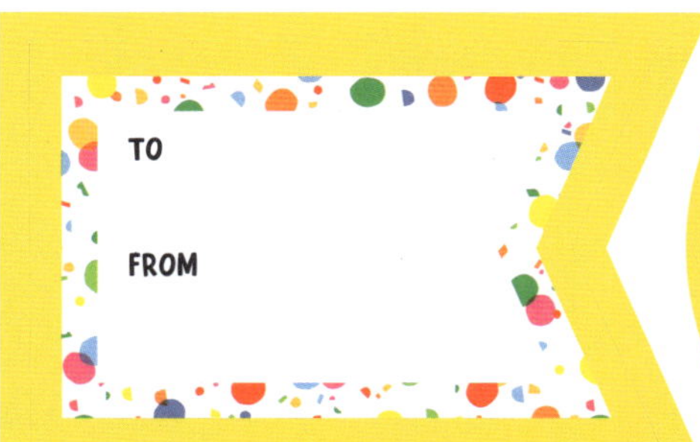
TO
FROM
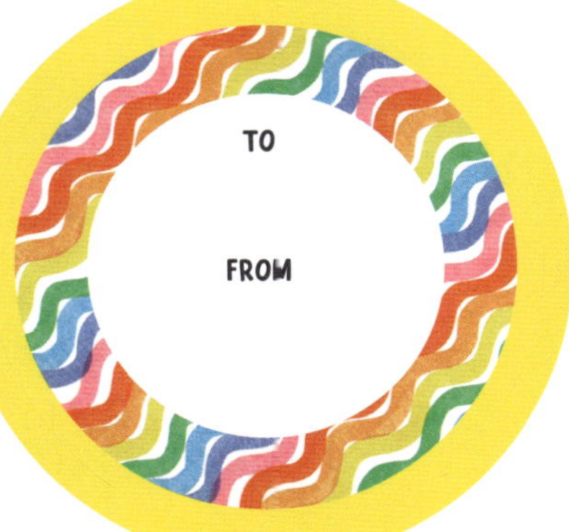
TO
FROM
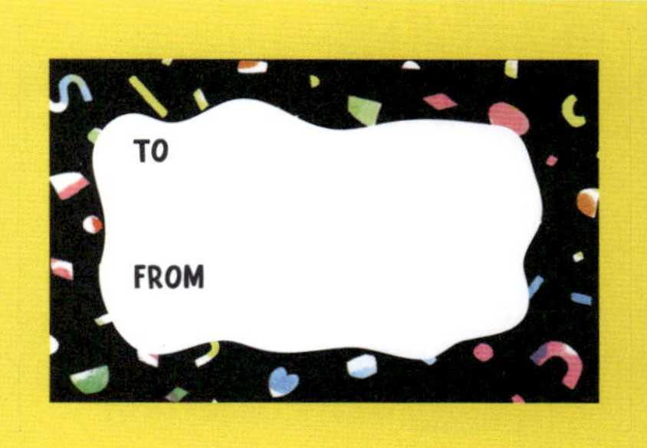
TO
FROM
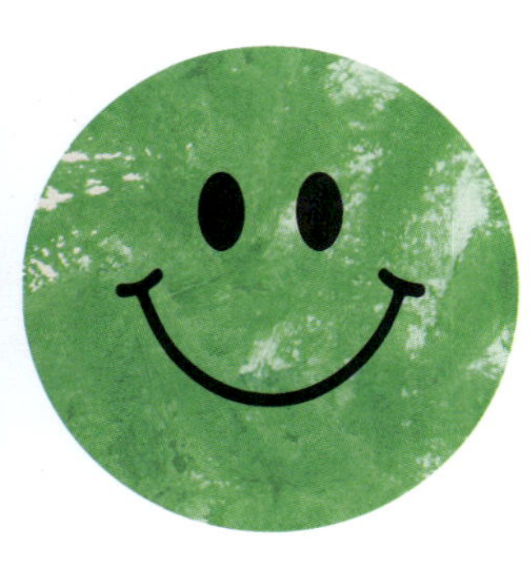
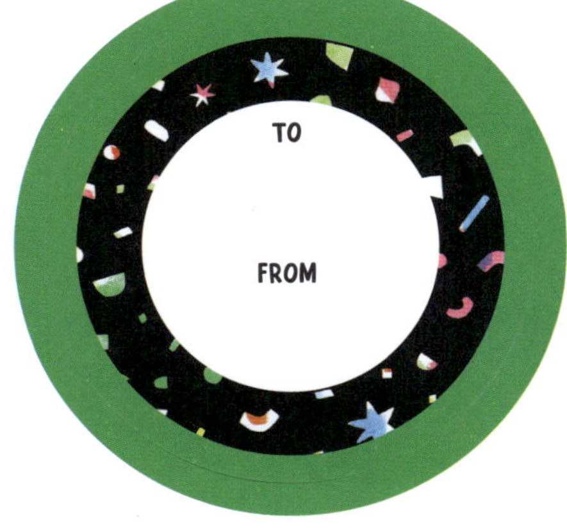
TO
FROM
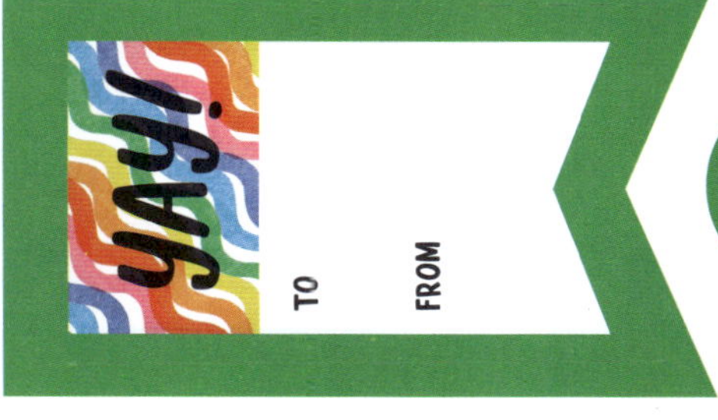
YAY!
TO
FROM
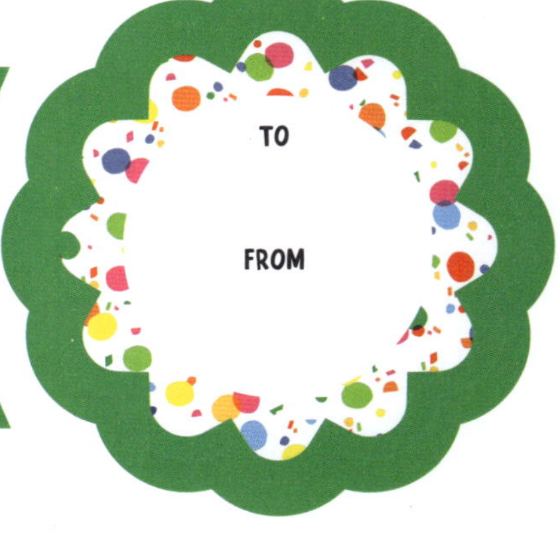
TO
FROM
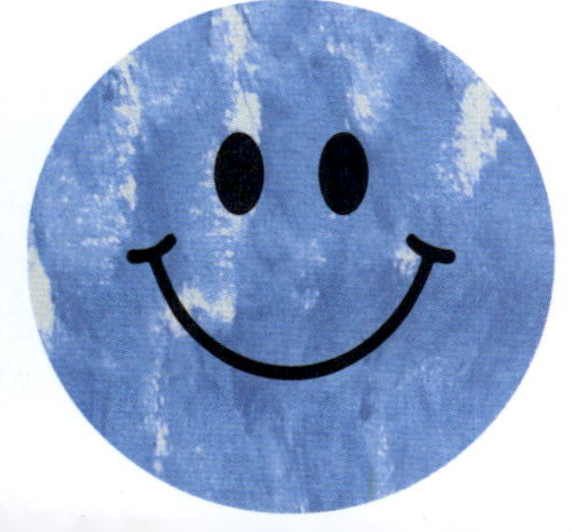
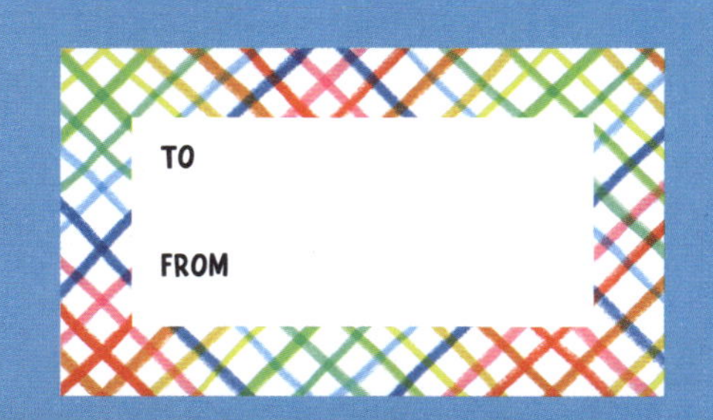
TO
FROM
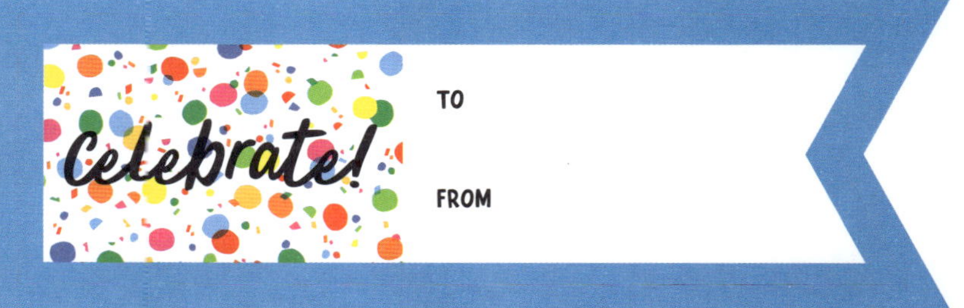
Celebrate!
TO
FROM

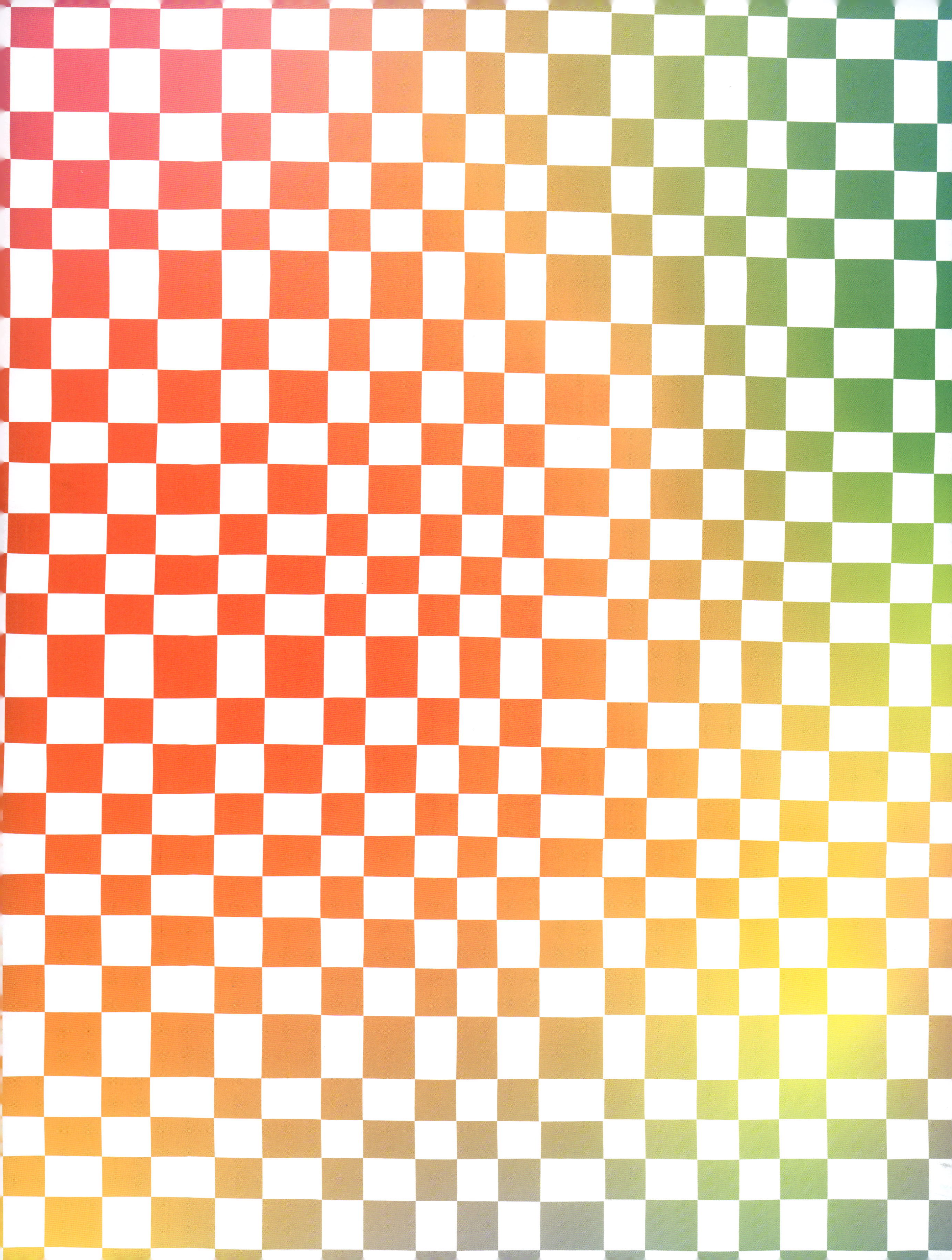

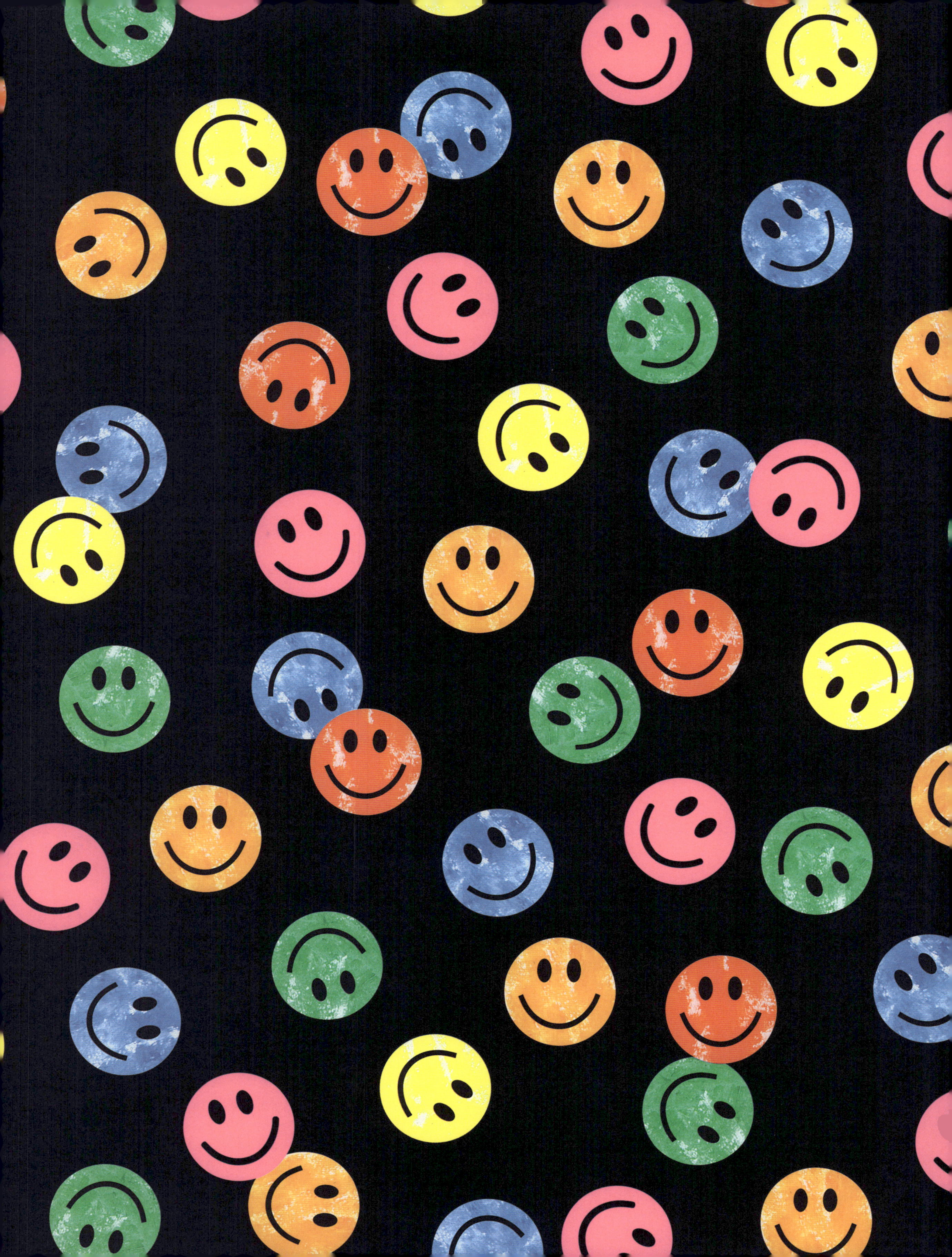

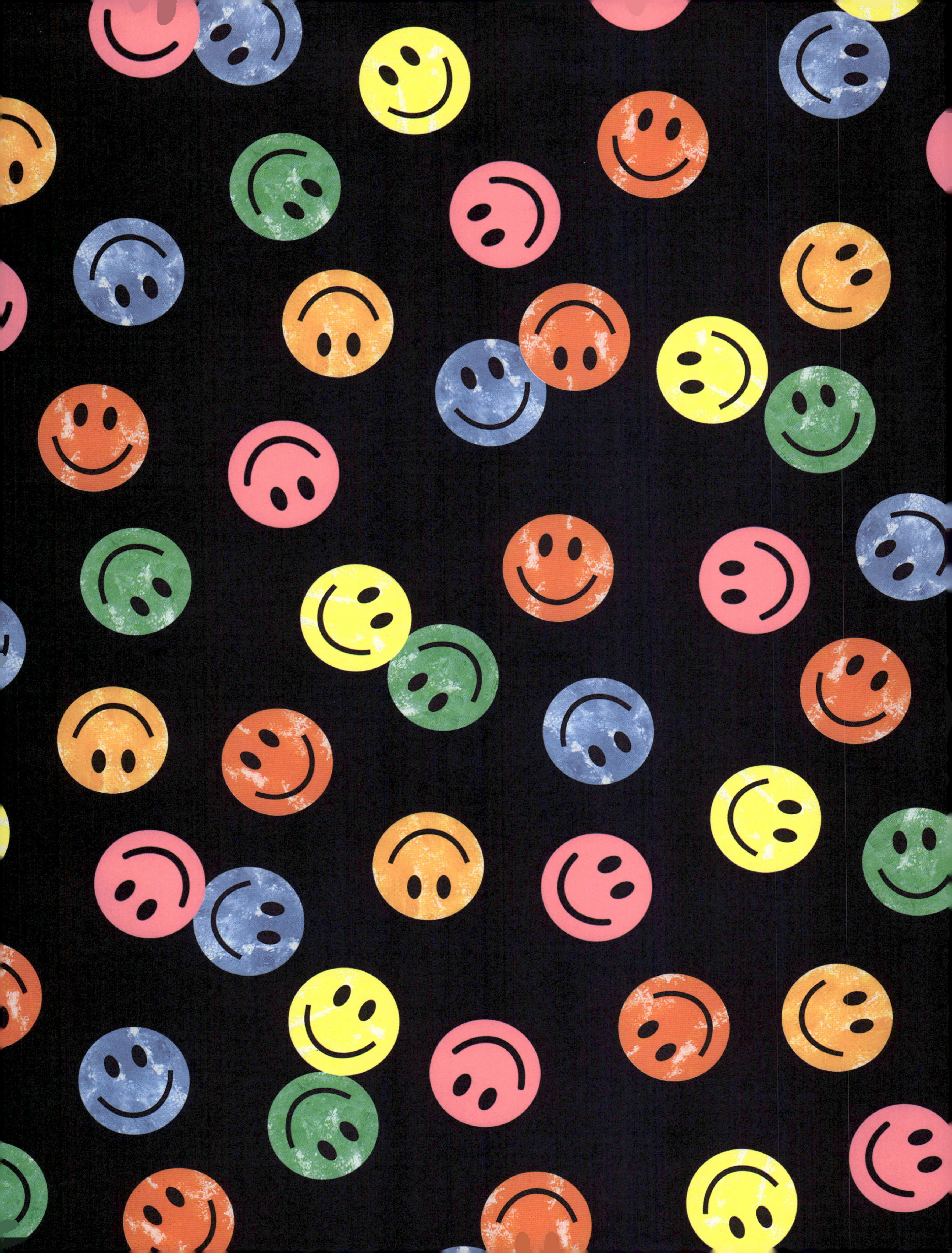

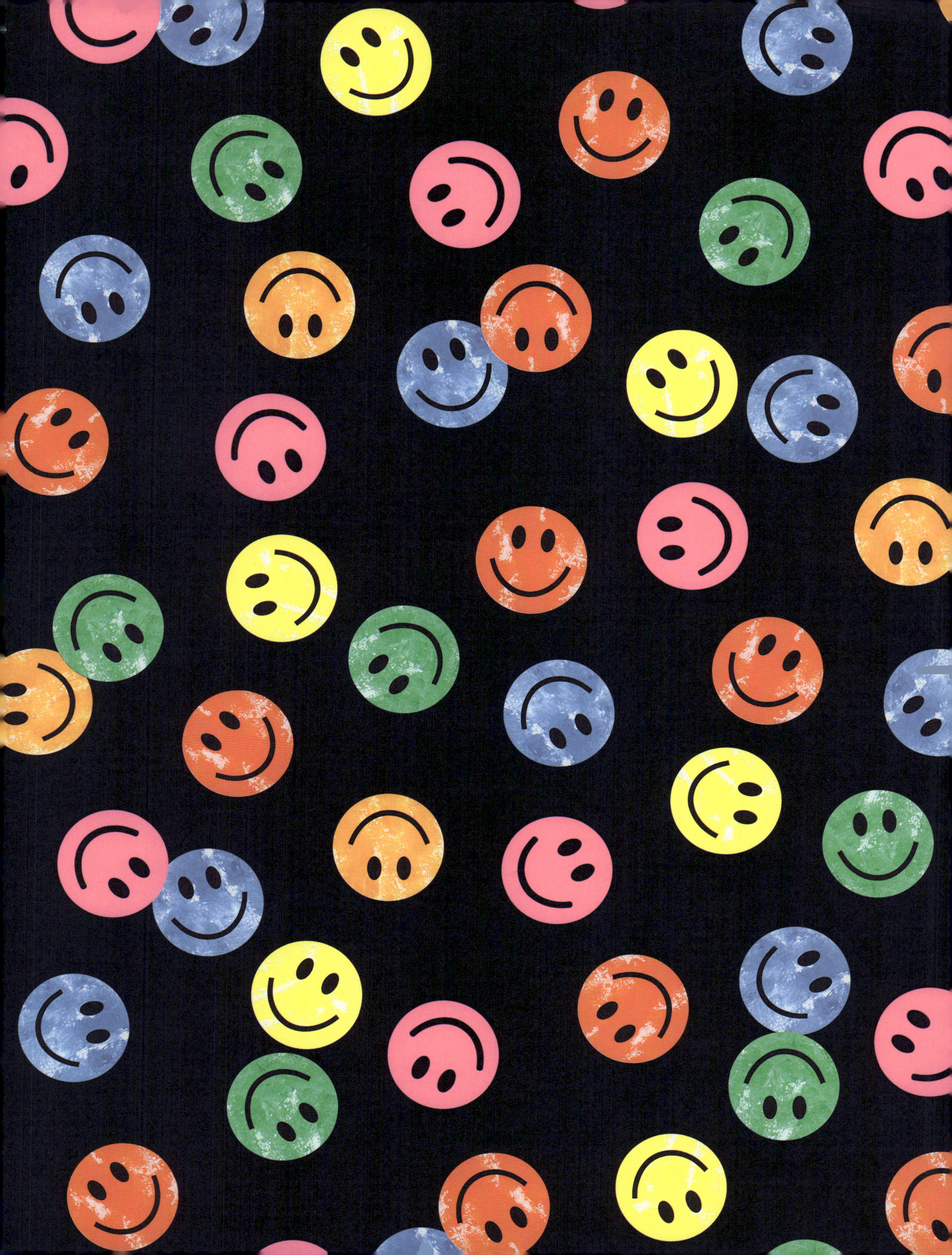

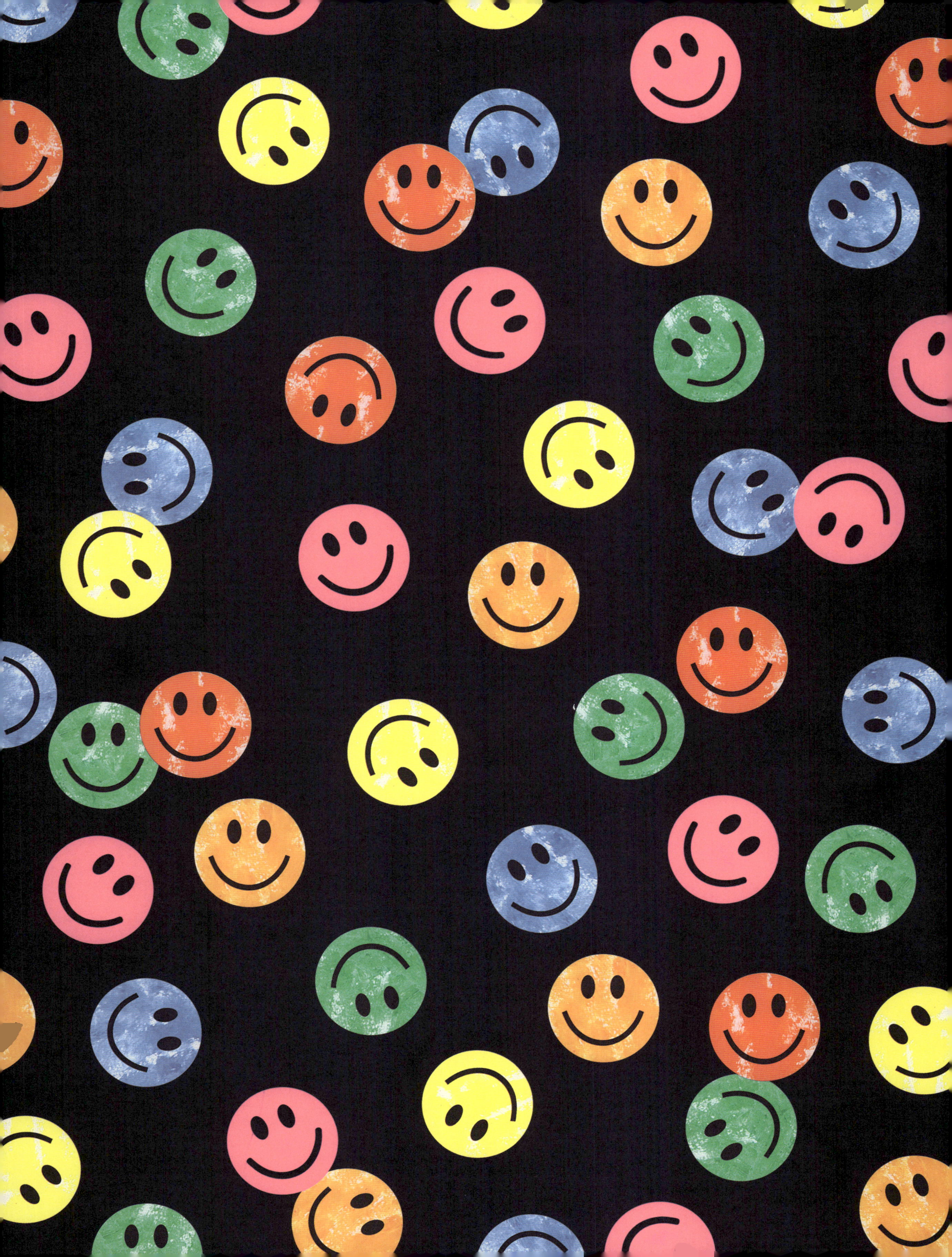

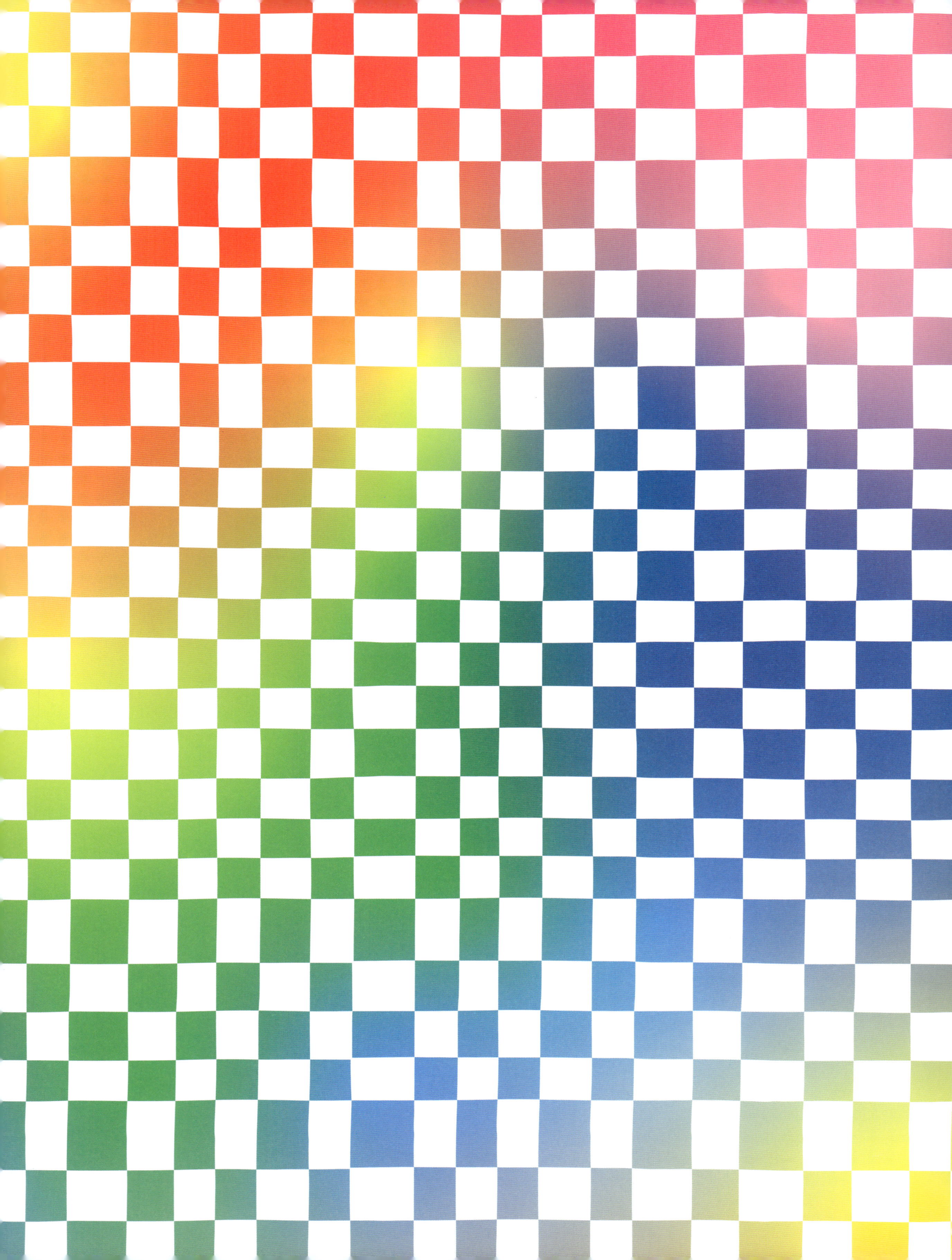

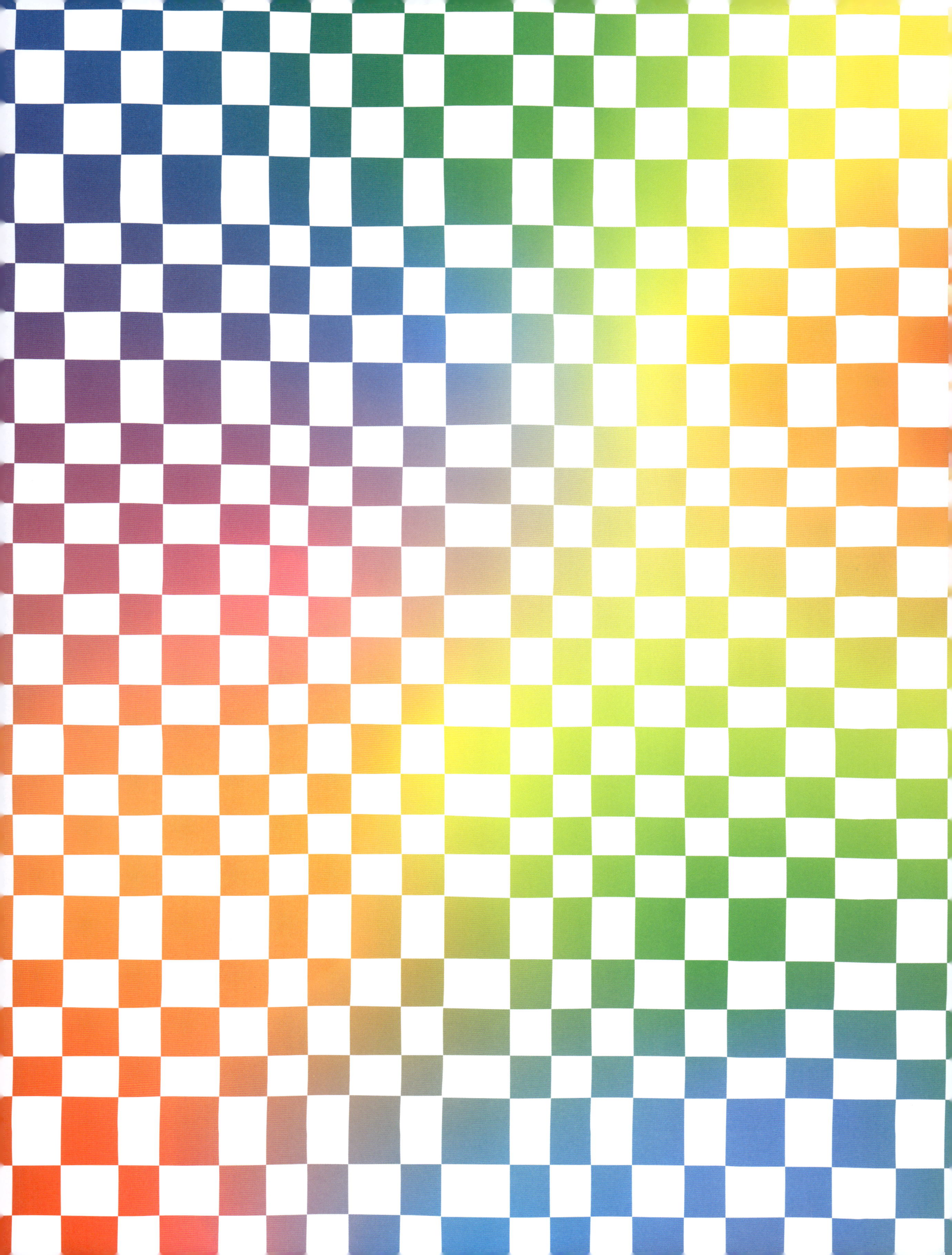